Salvation by Faith
and
Your Will

by
Morris L. Venden

Southern Publishing Association, Nashville, Tennessee

Library of Congress Cataloging in Publication Data

Venden, Morris L
   Salvation by faith and your will.

    1. Election (Theology)—Addresses, essays, lectures.
2. Salvation—Addresses, essays, lectures.   3. Freedom (Theology)—Addresses, essays, lectures.
4. Free will and determinism—Addresses, essays,
lectures. I. Title.
BT810.2.V45   234   78-7597
ISBN 0-8127-0190-9

Contents

Preface

In my years of ministry I have encountered one particular question again and again: "How do I use my will and my willpower in living the Christian life? What about the question of known sin? Where does my human effort end and where does God's divine power begin?"

Some of us have studied this frustrating—though rewarding—question for years. We have even at times felt tempted to scrap the whole study, but always we've been drawn back to it because of its unresolved questions.

The subject of the will contains a strange paradox. It is simple, and yet for many it is difficult. In the days of Christ the "good" people rejected its impact, but "sinners" welcomed it with joy. Spiritual death awaits those who misunderstand the subject. Those who grasp it find the secret of victorious Christian living.

While philosophers, theologians, and psychologists through the centuries have discussed, debated, and theorized about man's nature and free will versus determinism, they have placed little emphasis on the operation of the postconversion will. Probably this has occurred because of the two doctrines of predestination and "cheap grace," for neither belief attaches any importance to the human will. Luther and Erasmus, in the sixteenth century, dialogued on the freedom or enslavement of the will, but they focused primarily on the preconversion will.

Our denomination has written little on the subject, and our church apparently has no consensus on it. Some of us have tried to study the will in the writings of Ellen G. White, only to encounter apparent paradoxes or contradictions. One paragraph tells us that we can do nothing to save ourselves or to become sanctified except to keep coming to Christ just as we are. And another admonishes us to put forth strenuous effort, exerting every ounce of energy and self-discipline, instead of sitting around waiting for God to do our part for us. And we've debated among ourselves: Does God expect us only to rely totally upon Him in a personal relationship, or does He want us to put forth strenuous effort in addition?

For the past few years some of us have been studying this topic weekly, looking forward to the day when we would feel confident enough to present a series on the will. The following chapters, based on sermons first given at the La Sierra Seventh-day Adventist Church of Loma Linda University, are the result. Katherine Ching, of Loma Linda University, helped prepare them for publication. She edited and transformed them from taped sermons to book chapters.

This book is dedicated especially to those who have been born again into Christ, to those who are experiencing the joys and struggles of living the Christian life, to those who are becoming discouraged and ready to give up religion entirely because of continual defeat and failure in daily living. It is my prayer that an understanding of this topic will lead all of us to seek a closer personal fellowship with God each day.

M. L. V.

Chapter 1

A Modern Parable

In this book we will discuss many concepts that appear intangible and difficult to understand. The experience of using the human will properly, in the ongoing relationship with Christ, is progressive. Understanding of the theory and the experience does not happen overnight. Rather, each day we must learn to depend on God constantly, and not on our own resources for strength and power.

Because it is so difficult to explain the great principles of righteousness by faith in simple terms without getting involved in a debate over semantics, I will first try to describe the experience of "abiding in Christ" in terms of a modern parable.

My basis for such an approach appears in Jesus' own example. "And the disciples came, and said unto him, Why speakest thou unto them in parables? He answered and said unto them, Because it is given unto you to know the mysteries of the kingdom of heaven, but to them it is not given. For whosoever hath, to him shall be given, and he shall have more abundance: but whosoever hath not, from him shall be taken away even that he hath. Therefore speak I to them in parables: because they seeing see not; and hearing they hear not, neither do they understand" (Matthew 13:10-13).

Jesus used parables sometimes to hide and other times

to reveal. Because He addressed His audience in terms of pictures and language they could understand, I believe that if He spoke to us in person today, He'd talk about jet planes, electricity, highways, freeways, and cars. And so I would like to describe, in parable form, the Christian's life on earth as he grows in his relationship with God.

I was in the Empire State Building, riding the elevator to the top to have a look at the gleaming lights of the city below—the great New York City. At the sixty-sixth floor the door opened, and a famous billionaire walked in. It surprised me because I thought he was out of the country somewhere. Although I recognized him, I didn't want him to know, because it might make him nervous, and I was afraid he would vanish. Being alone in the elevator with him, I looked alternately at the walls and at him. As we continued on our journey to the top floor, he evidently noticed my gazing at him, for he suddenly broke the silence. "Do you know who I am?"

"I'm not sure, but you are certainly handsome!" I answered. (I wanted to make points with him!)

We reached the top floor, and as the door opened I made sure that he could get off the elevator first. Together we walked over to the edge of the rooftop and looked down at the street below. Evidently my behavior had impressed him, for he turned to me and said, "I have a proposition to make with you."

"Really?" I responded. I hoped it would involve money.

"Yes," he said. "I have a million dollars that I want to give you."

"You want to *give* me a million dollars?" Although I wondered what the catch was in his offer, I feared to offend him by asking. Besides, I had been wishing I had enough to buy a new Jaguar, and I figured that his offer would amply more than cover the cost. I was delighted.

But then he continued, "I want to give you the money on two conditions. The first is that you promise to spend the entire sum in one year."

Well, I would have preferred to spread out the fun over a longer period of time, but I also reasoned that it would be better to have one million to spend in one year than to have none at all. So I agreed.

"Good," he replied. "Now here is the second condition. At the end of the year, from wherever you are, whether you're in the Far East or the South Seas, whether you're in Acapulco or the Caribbean, you must promise to meet me here on the rooftop of the Empire State Building."

"Is that all?" I questioned. "What happens next?"

"You'll meet me here, and then you'll jump off this building to splat on the pavement below."

"Beg your pardon?" I gasped.

He repeated his condition. "If you do not jump—and there's no way you can get out of it; you can't use the million to get lost somewhere—then I'll push you from this same spot, and you'll still die at the end of one year."

It didn't take me much deliberation to turn to my would-be benefactor and say, "You know something? You're ugly!" I turned around and walked back to the elevator.

On the way down, I couldn't help thinking about his ridiculous offer, and I wondered if anyone in his right mind could ever accept such a deal. At the seventy-seventh floor a man dressed in white joined me. I thought I had seen him somewhere before—perhaps in pictures. He smiled and greeted me, but I felt reluctant to talk to him, feeling rather distrustful of people I met in elevators.

Somehow he didn't seem to mind my apprehensiveness. "I notice you've been admiring the lights of New York," he said.

"Yes," I replied cautiously; "it's certainly beautiful."

Then he began telling me about a fantastic city that was even better. It sounded unbelievable. One fifth larger than the state of Oregon, it had a most fantastic river running through it. As he described its fruit trees, I could almost taste the fruit. I could imagine the beauty of the scene.

"How do I get there?" I asked.

"You can find the way only through me," he replied, "but I'll be glad to take you there."

"How far is it?"

"It's a hundred five trillion miles."

A hundred five trillion miles! How could I ever get there in my lifetime? Just then the elevator stopped at the sixty-sixth floor, and another man got on. He resembled a magician—black suit, pitch-black beard and moustache, and a high hat that looked as though he were trying to hide something underneath. As my friend from the seventy-seventh floor continued to describe his city, the newcomer watched me with penetrating eyes, and finally he butted rudely into the conversation. My friend in white politely let him have the floor.

"I have a fabulous city too," he stated. "You should see the lights. At night you can hardly believe the beauty of the place. And the fun you can have starts whenever you arrive there. You don't have to wait."

"Well," I questioned, "how do I get there?"

"I'll show you the way."

"How far is it?"

"You can be there in four hours."

"*Four hours?*"

"Yes."

"Well, what are we waiting for? Let's go right now!" I cried.

We continued on down to the ground floor. While the man in white disappeared down the street, the one in black took me to the airport where we boarded an airplane and flew to Las Vegas, Nevada.

We got there at night. The lights were on, and I had more fun than I had ever imagined possible. Then I slept until noon the next day. Finally, when I was wide awake enough to look around, I started strolling aimlessly down the streets. To my surprise I saw a Jaguar agency that offered me a new Jaguar for $1 down and $1 a week. I could hardly believe those terms.

For a month I roared around Las Vegas, having a great time. But the strange thing was that after the fun ended, there was nothing left. And I discovered, much to my amazement, that all the things I did to have fun were enjoyable while they lasted—but they didn't last. Before long—thirty days, in fact—I was sick of it all. I wanted happiness, something deeper and more lasting, and in complete frustration I left the town.

Out on the edge of town, I looked at the signposts and noticed the name of the same city that my friend from the seventy-seventh floor of the Empire State Building had described to me. Sure enough—the sign said that it was a hundred five trillion miles away. But this time I didn't care about the distance. I decided that I was going to get there if it was the last thing I did. Revving up my engine, I headed down the freeway away from Vegas, toward the direction of the city. The four-lane freeway was lovely—even though it didn't have a center divider. I decided to drive as fast as possible so that I could get to my destination quickly.

But soon after I headed down the freeway, I discovered something terrible. All of the traffic came against me, headed toward Vegas. It was like driving the wrong way on a one-way street. Only rarely did a few cars seem to be going my direction. In fact, because of all the cars racing toward Vegas, I couldn't carry out my original plan of cruising at ninety miles an hour. Instead, I had to edge over on the shoulder, for some of the traffic was way over on my side. And while on the shoulder, I kept going slower and slower—70, 60, 40, 30, 20 miles an hour. Everybody knows that you can't get to a destination a hundred five trillion miles away at twenty miles an hour.

To make things even worse, as I drove along the shoulder one day, around the bend up ahead loomed a huge diesel truck—a Peterbilt loaded with logs. He swung right over to my side of the highway, onto the shoulder, and headed straight for me, ignoring the honking of my horn. Now, I didn't like the idea of a head-on collision with a diesel truck. So just before we hit, I drove off the shoulder into the ditch. Gravel and dirt scattered about as I came to a halt, and the fenders on my Jaguar were scratched up. For a while I sat there, discouraged with the prospects of ever arriving at that distant city, but my friend's description of its beauty kept going through my mind. "I'd better keep on trying," I said to myself; so I pulled out of the ditch and headed onto the freeway again, hoping to make better time. But the traffic was still impossible, and once more I had to crawl on the shoulder at twenty miles an hour. Every few days another of those diesel trucks would roar around the bend. The next one carried a load of hay, headed straight for me. Again I ended up in the ditch.

The journey continued—a constant nightmare of going in and out of the ditch. One day as I sat in the ditch, thinking of giving up on the whole idea, ready to forget trying to reach the city, I heard a knock on my window. The sound surprised me because I hadn't seen any hitchhiker on the road. When I looked out, much to my joy I saw my friend in white from the seventy-seventh floor. Opening the door, I greeted him. He said, "Would you like me to drive for you?"

Not being sure if he knew all the hazards of the route, I asked, "Have you been over this road?"

"Yes, I've traveled this way before."

"Well," I sighed, "I'm sure making a mess of this trip. I'd very much like for you to drive for me."

When I slid over to the passenger's side, he moved in and took the wheel. As he drove out onto the freeway his sleeve fell back and I saw a big, muscular arm. "What kind of work have you been doing most of your life, anyway?" I asked.

"I've been working in a cabinet shop."

And then he headed down the freeway at ninety miles an hour. He didn't drive on the shoulder, either. Unable to believe it, I just sat there in amazement. The Datsuns, the Volkswagens, the Hondas, the Lincoln Continentals, the Chrysler Imperials—all seemed to stay out of his way. "Ninety miles an hour . . . !" I said to myself, "I think we'll make it to that city after all." Overjoyed, I wanted to shout out the window, "You should see my driver!" A spontaneous desire to let everyone know about him filled me.

And then one day as we sped along, around the bend up ahead came another of those impossible diesel trucks. It made no difference who drove my car—the truck headed straight for us. Not liking the idea of a head-on collision with a diesel truck at ninety miles an hour, I made a lunge for the steering wheel before we got any closer. My driver made no objection when I took the wheel. He moved right over. I whipped the wheel around as fast as I could, the tires screeched, and we careened into the ditch.

Ditching a car at ninety miles an hour is not advisable. In fact, the gravel almost turned the car over, and the fenders got smashed in as we spun around, but somehow we missed the truck. And when the dust had settled, I discovered my driver was still in the car with me. He tapped my shoulder and asked, "Would you like me to drive again?"

"How can we drive this thing?" I asked. "The fenders are bashed in against the wheels."

"Don't worry," he replied. "I know how to fix them." Much to my surprise he was an excellent body-and-fender man. Now, where he ever learned that type of work in a cabinet shop, I don't know.

Soon the fenders were out, and we headed down the freeway again—at ninety miles an hour. As he drove, I said to myself, "Now he *did* tell me that he'd been over this road already. He must have met diesels before." And I began to wonder what I'd do if we ever met another one of those trucks.

We journeyed along for several days. I learned that my driver never forced himself upon me. At any time I could take over the driving. But each morning as we started our day's trip he asked me if I wanted him to stay with me and drive, and I always said, "Yes."

One day another diesel truck loaded with hay came around the bend. "Now look here," I said to myself. "Keep your cool. Don't do anything stupid. Keep your grubby little hands off the steering wheel. He knows how to handle diesel trucks. Stay out of his way!" But I didn't feel like doing *nothing*. I wanted to do something myself. Yet, since he *had* told me that he knew the road from before, I thought, "Let him handle this."

I closed my eyes and opened them again. I chewed my nails. I fussed with the seat belt. What made the whole situation worse to me was that as my driver got closer to the diesel, he accelerated to 120 miles an hour. It took every ounce of willpower, self-discipline, energy, and human effort that I had to sit there. Have you ever heard the expression, "Don't just stand there—do something!"? It's really difficult to change it the other way around: "Don't just do something, sit there."*

Somehow I managed to let him remain in charge, and just before we would have collided head-on, *the diesel went in the ditch.* I couldn't believe it. And as we sped by I caught a glimpse of the driver. It was the man from the sixty-sixth floor, the one who had flown me to Vegas, and he had a pitchfork beside him in the cab—for loading hay.

Really excited, I thanked my driver. Now I had even more reason to shout out the window, "You should see my driver! He can meet anything on this road." I even wanted to get bumper stickers that said, "Honk if you know my driver."

We continued the journey day after day. It was a wonderful experience for a while. But then to my surprise, I began to get bored with the countryside, frustrated from not doing the driving. I got impatient and tired of the trip. Naturally I didn't like to keep admitting that I couldn't do the driving. It damaged my ego. And I wanted to protest, "I know how to drive. I'm a big boy now. I've been to drivers' school." Leaving my driver in control was turning out to be a crucifying experience. I was tired of all the effort that it took to let him do the driving for me. Furthermore, up ahead, I saw an amusement park off to the left side. It looked like a fabulous place—it had things like Matterhorn bobsleds and jungle boat rides and more. Although I wanted to stop, I was quite sure that my driver wouldn't turn off to that road. So I tapped him on the shoulder and

---

*This parable is *not* meant to teach a "do-nothing" religion. The truth is that the car represents me, a person. The driver is in control of the person by the individual's own choice. It doesn't make the person inactive, but extremely active (Galatians 2:20). For the old-fashioned version of this parable read *Life Sketches*, pages 190-193.

said, "Pardon me. May I drive?"

He never kept me from driving, never took my power of choice away from me, and never made any objection whenever I asked to take over. When he slipped out of the driver's seat, I grabbed the wheel. To my surprise, the Datsuns and the VWs stayed out of my way. Slowing down to a turning speed, I swung left, down the road toward the amusement park. Coming around a curve I hadn't anticipated in time, I drove off a cliff.

Down at the bottom of the cliff as I returned to consciousness, with bolts and engine parts falling around me, my companion tapped me on the shoulder and said, "Would you like me to drive again?"

And I said, "As a matter of fact, the thought had crossed my mind."

I don't know how he did it, but somehow he put the body and fenders of my car back together again and got the engine running. Before long we headed down the freeway at ninety miles an hour again. "Licking my wounds," I determined never to take the wheel again. My driver never reproached me for my foolishness.

But as we went along, day after day, I suddenly found myself in the driver's seat without even realizing that I had gotten there. I didn't know how it happened. In fact, I didn't even notice I was driving at first because the other small cars stayed out of my way. But then I saw another diesel roaring around the bend up ahead, and whenever I saw those diesels, I'd always ask myself who was doing the driving. Realizing that I was, the thought crossed my mind: "You saw how he did it. Why can't you do the same? Step it up to 120 miles an hour and head straight for the truck. That'll make him go into the ditch!"

The challenge made me feel really good, because, after all, I'd had a firsthand lesson on how to handle the diesel.

So I hung onto the wheel and accelerated up to 120. I don't need to tell you the rest. We collided head-on. I would have lost my life in the horrible crash, but just before the impact, my friend threw himself over in front of me, and *he* ended up bruised and bleeding.

After the debris had settled around me, he said, "Want me to drive?"

"Drive *what?*" I asked.

But to my surprise I found again that he was not only a cabinetmaker and a body-fender man but a master mechanic as well. Once more we headed down the freeway toward the distant city—with my driver behind the wheel. As I looked at his bruises and bleeding wounds I felt heartbroken and asked him to forgive me.

Little by little, as we travel on together, I realize that I fail whenever I try to help him do what he has already promised to do—driving for me and getting me to that city. My failures always come, not because I don't try hard enough to drive, but because I fail to let *him* drive for me. Whenever a diesel approaches, whether it's loaded with logs or hay or coal, if I happen to be in the driver's seat by mistake or by deliberate choice, I repent and let him take over quick. I notice something else begins to happen too. I discover that the other cars begin to look like diesels as well.

The journey isn't over yet, but just the other day we came to a fork in the road. One road went off to the left and ended in a sunken garden, beautiful beyond description— flowers, golf course, green lawns, fountains, lakes and streams, waving palm trees. It had a wide, eight-lane causeway going into it. But the fork to the right went off the main pavement onto some gravel, and then, up ahead, I could see chuckholes going on a weaving pattern up the mountain.

Which road did my driver take? He took the road to the right—the one with the chuckholes. I tapped him on the shoulder and said, "Did you see the other road?"

"Yes."

"Are you sure you're on the right one? The other way looked more like your description of the distant city."

"I'm sure I'm on the right road. But if you don't think so, you may drive."

"No, please, you keep on."

As we continued to wind our way up the mountain, back and forth, higher and higher, I glanced back at those beautiful sunken gardens, and just on the other side I saw huge billows of smoke rolling up. It resembled the smoke from burning Peterbilt diesels and pitchforks and hay.

Now I am determined to leave my driver behind the steering wheel as we continue to climb the narrow chuckhole road. But something exciting has been happening. From the other side of the mountain glows a glorious light. I can hardly wait to see what it is. It is a most fantastic light, and I get clearer glimpses of it as we come nearer. I have an idea that it must be from that distant city. In the meantime, although I'm no less interested in that city, I'm having a great time getting better acquainted with my driver, and as I learn to know him more and more, I increasingly love and trust him.

Chapter 2

What Man Can Do

While it may appear dull and unimportant on the surface, the operation of the human will after the initial conversion experience is the pivot point around which the entire understanding of *imparted* righteousness by faith turns. Yet a study of the subject reveals it to be one of the most easily misunderstood aspects of the great theme of sanctification by faith. And it is probably also one of the most frustrating topics to study, because we have made it that way. We discover in the end that it is one of the simplest basic truths to living the Christian life.

The frustration began for me several years ago when I read through the book *Steps to Christ*, determined to find all the answers. On page 18 I came across the statement: "Education, culture, the exercise of the will, human effort, all have their proper sphere, but here they are powerless." I didn't quite grasp its context, but I got the idea that the will and human effort had limited powers.

Continuing, I came to page 47, which declared, "What you need to understand is the true force of the will." And I said, "Beg your pardon? I don't get it. Earlier I learned that the will was powerless, but now I discover that I need to understand its force." To my bewildered mind, it sounded like double-talk. How could a powerless will have any force? In ignorance, I began to try developing more willpower, reasoning that if the force of the will was important, then I needed to have more force to my will. So I tried to develop more willpower or backbone by compelling myself to do things I did not want to do or found difficult to do—getting up at three o'clock in the morning; drinking sixteen glasses of water without stopping; staying out of the cookie jar; not eating between meals. I was really developing willpower—so I thought. But I ended up in great trouble, realizing that all my efforts were futile.

My frustration led me to study further into the subject of the will. Some people cautioned, "Don't study it. You'll get too analytical, too detailed. Just remember God loves you—that's all that matters." Our usual tendency is to leave the typical struggling Christian to find out how to use his will by accident, assuming that he'll stumble onto the solution someday. But that's no answer.

At one time I decided to scrap the whole study because it didn't seem I'd ever be able to figure out the answers. But then I'd be brought back because of such statements as these: "What you need to understand is the true force of the will" (*Steps to Christ*, p. 47); "You will be in constant peril until you understand the true force of the will" (*Testimonies for the Church*, Vol. 5, p. 513); "Through the right exercise of the will, an entire change may be made in the life" (*The Ministry of Healing*, p. 176).

So I proceeded to try to understand the proper relation between divine power and human effort. And I became more certain that the subject of the will is central and pivotal in the great theme of salvation by faith. It is one thing to understand its general principles in *theory*; it is another to grasp the concept of the part that the human will plays in everyday experience.

I began my study by turning to the Bible. To my amazement I found that even Bible characters endured many years of problems and difficulties before they understood the proper use of their wills.

After the Flood God promised that He would never again destroy the earth in that manner. Some believed His promise. Others did not. Those who doubted His word began to build a tower just in case God wouldn't keep His promise. The tower project failed.

Abraham had a similar experience. God led him to a land that he would receive as an inheritance and further promised him that he would be the father of a great multitude. When he arrived in Canaan after a long journey, the people greeted him:

"Welcome to our land. What's your name?"

"My name is 'Father of a Multitude,' " he replied, because that was what his name meant.

"Oh," they said, "your name means 'Father of a Multitude'? How many children do you have?"

"Well, . . . I don't have any." And the people smiled.

They met Sarah. "Welcome to Canaan. What's your name?"

"My name is 'Mother of Nations.' "

"Oh, it is! How many children do *you* have?"

"Well, . . . I don't have any children."

Then the people took a little closer look at Sarah and asked, "How old are you, anyway?"

"I'm sixty-five." And that was even more embarrassing.

Finally Abraham decided that God must have made a promise He couldn't keep. "He needs our help," he concluded. Abraham and Sarah discussed the problem together and came up with a plan that seemed acceptable according to the customs of their day. Soon a tragic family situation developed. Only after years of heartache did Abraham finally learn the lesson that would qualify him for the name "Father of the Faithful."

God told Moses to lead Israel out of the land of Egypt to the *Promised* Land. Moses said, "All right, if I am the man you want, I might as well get started." He started swinging his sword and killed one Egyptian. Then he fled into the wilderness, where for forty years, as he herded sheep, he learned the lesson of faith and the will. At the end of forty years God reminded him that he was to lead Israel out of Egypt.

Moses replied, "I can't do it. I'm a born sheepherder. It's impossible for *me* to deliver Israel." But now God knew he was ready, for Moses was finally willing to depend on divine power.

Then in spite of their wonderful leader, who had learned the hard way, Israel went through the same experience. They had the promise, "The Lord your God he shall fight for you" (Deuteronomy 3:22). But Israel wandered in the wilderness for forty years, trying to absorb the same lesson that Moses had had to learn before them—that when God makes a promise, He has the power to keep it, and He does not need our interference. Our meddling merely hinders Him from accomplishing His purposes.

Remember when Peter declared to Jesus, "Though I should die with thee, yet will I not deny thee" (Matthew 26:35)? Peter made the right choice, but he did not have the power to back it up. Only a few hours later he found himself defeated and fleeing from the mob. He did not understand the proper function of the will.

When I read Romans 7, I found comfort and courage because I realized that even the apostle Paul with his great spiritual insight and giant intellect had difficulty understanding the will. He describes his frustrations in trying to live the Christian life: "That which I do I allow not: for that I would do, that do I not; but what I hate, that do I. If then I do that which I would not, I consent unto the law that it is good. Now then it is no more I that do it, but sin that dwelleth in me. For I know that in me (that is, in my flesh,) dwelleth no good thing: *for to will is present with me; but how to perform that which is good I find not.* For the good that I would I do not: but the evil which I would not, that I do" (Romans 7:15-19). Paul knew how to will or to choose the right thing, but he couldn't carry through in practice. Evidently he suffered defeat and failure in his Christian life. He says, "What's wrong? I *will* to do, but I can't perform."

Of course, some will argue that Paul speaks of his life before initial conversion, when he first came to Christ, but is there any difference in the operation of the will pre- and post-conversion? "As ye have therefore received Christ Jesus the Lord, so walk ye in him" (Colossians 2:6). *Steps to Christ*, page 69, tells us that we are to "abide" in Christ in the same way that we first received Him. So although I am taking the position that Paul describes a converted person's frustrations, the same principles would apply to the operation of the preconversion will. The will would function the same in justification as in sanctification.

Paul also makes this famous statement concerning the will in Philippians 2:12: "Wherefore, my beloved, as ye have always obeyed, not as in my presence only, but now much more in my absence, work out your own salvation with fear and trembling." If you were to stop here, the text would seem to support those who are trying to get to heaven by their good works. But Paul continues in the next verse, "For it is God which worketh in you both to will and to do of his good pleasure."

Does this contradict something he said in Romans 4? "Now to him that worketh is the reward not reckoned of grace, but of debt. But to him that worketh not, but believeth on him that justifieth the ungodly, his faith is counted for righteousness" (verses 4, 5). In one passage he says that we must work, but in another he declares that faith, not works, saves us. And the only way to harmonize the two is to conclude that while we have to work on *something* in the Christian life, there is also something that we're not supposed to work on.

Philippians 2:13 seems to indicate that God works in us. But right here a problem arises, because we can read the verse different ways. Notice the possibilities:

1. "For it is *God* which worketh in you both to will and to do of his good pleasure."
2. "For it is God which worketh in *you* both to will and to do of his good pleasure."
3. "For it is *God* which worketh in *you both to will and to do* of his good pleasure."

Do you see the differences?

Which one is right? What has been your experience? Does *God* work in you to will and to do—does *He* do the willing and the doing in you if you'll let Him? Or do *you* have to will and do in addition to the relationship? Herein lies the fine line between faith and works. And if we're not careful, it becomes a giant chasm.

For years, the majority position in our church has apparently been justification by faith alone and sanctification by faith plus works. We've gotten the idea that victorious living requires something we have to do ourselves *in addition* to faith. But is this correct? Notice another text by the same author on sanctification: "May the God of peace himself sanctify you wholly; and may your spirit and soul and body be kept sound and blameless at the coming of our Lord Jesus Christ. *He who calls you is faithful, and he will do it*" (1 Thessalonians 5:23, 24, RSV). Right here

I'd like to suggest the way we shall interpret Philippians 2:13: "For it is *God* which worketh in you *both to will and to do* of his good pleasure."

Now, some people will resist and oppose such a conclusion because it threatens their false security and deflates their egos. But let me remind you that justification by faith is "the work of God in laying the glory of man in the dust, and doing for man that which it is not in his power to do for himself" (*Testimonies to Ministers*, p. 456).

Someone might ask, "But what is it that we have the power to do, and what are we unable to do?" Therefore understanding our limitations and abilities becomes crucial. Wouldn't it be too bad to spend all your time and energy toward something at which you can never succeed, while ignoring that at which you can? Here is the reason we have so many discouraged Christians. We fail because we have not properly understood the operation of the human will, and as a result, the Christian church has become filled with people strong enough to conform outwardly, to be moral externally. Somehow we have gotten the idea that if we can be good enough, then we are Christians. But living the Christian life involves primarily the inward man, and if he is "good" inwardly, then his outward acts of goodness will follow naturally.

According to Webster, morality is "conforming to right principles of conduct, practice, or action." He also defines moralism as "the practice of morality *as distinct from religion*." Notice that he places religion and morality into two different camps. I could quote a similar statement by an inspired writer: "Many who call themselves Christians are mere human moralists" (*Christ's Object Lessons*, p. 315).

Of course it does not mean that a religious life will lead to immorality. Actually, true spirituality is the only thing that will produce a genuinely moral life. But the world has a substitute for real morality, a counterfeit known as conformity to right conduct and principles.

What can man do? What are his inherent capabilities and limitations? Perhaps the key to understanding the will is in the proper comprehension of man's nature. The Bible gives us plenty of descriptions: all are unrighteous (Romans 3:10) and "all unrighteousness is sin" (1 John 5:17). Romans 3:10-12, 23 declares, "There is none righteous, no, not one: there is none that understandeth, there is none that seeketh after God. They are all gone out of the way, they are together become unprofitable; there is none that doeth good, no, not one. . . . For all have sinned, and come short of the glory of God."

Other texts present similar viewpoints. "The carnal mind is enmity against God: for it is not subject to the law of God, neither indeed can be" (Romans 8:7); "if we say that we have no sin, we deceive ourselves, and the truth is not in us" (1 John 1:8); we are born in sin (Psalm 51:5); we are "by nature the children of wrath" (Ephesians 2:3); "all our righteousnesses [or morality] are as filthy rags" (Isaiah 64:6); we are full of "putrifying sores" (Isaiah 1:6); "in my flesh . . . dwelleth no good thing" (Romans 7:18); and "the heart is deceitful above all things, and desperately wicked" (Jeremiah 17:9).

Our hearts, not necessarily our outward actions, are sinful—our inherent natures are in a state of sin. And remember that God looks at the heart (1 Samuel 16:7). All of us are born with sinful natures—separated from God. We're sinners from birth. Sure, a baby doesn't have a desire to steal and smoke and drink and carouse. An infant doesn't commit all the acts which we term "sins," but he does have the one problem that is the root of all sin—selfishness. And we manage to teach him how to be more selfish. That's why Jesus says we must be born again

(John 3:3)—because something is wrong with our original birth.

Now that we know we are sinful, what are we supposed to do about it? *Can* we do anything about it? "It is impossible for us, of ourselves, to escape from the pit of sin in which we are sunken. Our *hearts* are evil, and we cannot change them" (*Steps to Christ*, p. 18). None of us, weak and strong alike, can transform our natures. Neither the weak nor the strong has the advantage when it comes to the *inner* man. And here is the context of the first statement I encountered when reading *Steps to Christ* to find the answers. " 'The carnal mind is enmity against God.' . . . Education, culture, the exercise of the will, human effort, all have their proper sphere, but here they are powerless" (*ibid.*). What are they powerless to do? "They may produce an *outward* correctness of behavior, *but they cannot change the heart; they cannot purify the springs of life*" (*ibid.*, italics supplied). Positive thinking, lifting myself up by my bootstraps, and all the rest of the man-made gimmicks we've come up with are useless when it comes to changing the *heart* of man. Apart from the renewing power of God and His Spirit, man cannot alter his heart. He can create only outward goodness.

While *some* men can produce externally correct behavior, others can't even do that much. The ones who can't conform to the laws of society wind up in prison—righteousness by incarceration. I remember attending college with such a person. He got into tremendous problems that went on and on for years, until he eventually spent more time in jail than out of it. Living nearby, I tried to help him and visited for hours in jail working with him. But whenever he'd get out, he'd go right back to his old problems. Finally in desperation I told him, "You know, my friend, you might be one of those people who will be able to go to heaven only straight from jail." I don't know how I could have said it. It wasn't very encouraging to him at the time. But years later I was overjoyed to receive a letter from him describing how he had come at last to that place that so many of us have difficulty reaching—the point where he realized that he couldn't help himself and where he turned his life over to God.

He had finally allowed God to catch up with him after coming to the end of his human resources, which were pitifully small in the first place. Having married a fine Christian, he was now a church leader. I still can hardly believe it, but it's true. It's thrilling to know that God can save the most hopeless, the most impossible cases. And I would like to say that doubtless he did not know the power of God to change him until he understood the right action of the will through experience, if not in theory.

Others would never get close to a jail. They're extremely moral people with backbones of steel, but they're not necessarily Christians, because, remember, moralists can behave correctly, outwardly, without God. "There may be an outward correctness of deportment without the renewing power of Christ. The love of influence and the desire for the esteem of others may produce a well-ordered life. Self-respect may lead us to avoid the appearance of evil. A selfish heart may perform generous actions" (*ibid.*, p. 58).

Then how are we supposed to know whose side we're on? Certainly not by our behavior alone. I could come to a church community, trying to set up a local shoe store, for example. And when I realized that most of my potential customers are church members, it would be wise for me to conform to their principles and maybe even join their church. Why? Because I could get more business that way. I could follow right principles for all sorts of evil motives, selfishly hoping I'd earn a reward. I could do all of the right things for the wrong reasons, and only God would know where my heart really is. Others might think that I'm a genuine Christian, but God knows better.

If the strongest person in the world, the one with the greatest self-discipline, cannot really change his *heart* one iota, then what benefits result from being moral? Certainly there are some, but salvation is not one of them, and neither is being a Christian. Being moral or outwardly good will never save a person, for it is possible for some to achieve it without a relationship with God (Philippians 3:6).

But even if a person can keep out of the physical jails of our world, he faces another prison from which he cannot escape. And its keeper never voluntarily opens his prison house. *Someone else* has to release the prisoners. An example appears in the Book of Mark. It tells of something exciting that happened in the synagogue one day. How would you like to be in church when a man comes running down the aisle, screaming, shouting, shaking his fist, foaming at the mouth, and wallowing on the floor? It has happened on occasion, and this time it happened in the presence of Jesus Himself:

"And they went into Capernaum; and straightway on the sabbath day he entered into the synagogue, and taught. And they were astonished at his doctrine: for he taught them as one that had authority, and not as the scribes. And there was in their synagogue a man with an unclean spirit; and he cried out, saying, Let us alone; what have we to do with thee, thou Jesus of Nazareth? art thou come to destroy us? I know thee who thou art, the Holy One of God. And Jesus rebuked him, saying, Hold thy peace, and come out of him. And when the unclean spirit had torn him, and cried with a loud voice, he came out of him. And they were all amazed, insomuch that they questioned among themselves, saying, What thing is this? what new doctrine is this? for with authority commandeth he even the unclean spirits, and they do obey him" (Mark 1:21-27).

I've often wondered about the difference between devil possession and insanity, for I've met some mentally ill people who exhibited all the symptoms of devil possession. At various times I have asked doctors, psychologists, and psychiatrists if perhaps any mental illness of a nonphysiological nature would be devil possession, but they won't all go along with that. However, in this case at least, insanity and devil possession were the same. His eyes "glared with the fire of insanity" (*The Desire of Ages*, p. 256).

Is it possible that many of us are devil possessed or mentally ill, even if no one has put us in institutions? I suppose you've heard or even used the expression, "I think all the world is 'touched' except thee and me, and sometimes I wonder about thee." Here we see, I'm sure, the epitome of pride. However, any person who lives a life apart from God will face the problem of possession or control by the devil. "Every man is free to choose what power he will have to rule over him" (*ibid.*, p. 258). Does that mean we have to have a power ruling over us? Yes. Can't we stay on neutral ground? No. "Unless we do yield ourselves to the control of Christ, we shall be dominated by the wicked one" (*ibid.*, p. 324). There is no middle ground.

The other day I talked to a formerly devil-possessed girl. She had gotten involved in the occult, and by her own voluntary choice had gone deeper and deeper into it. Everything happened to her. She seemed to enjoy the thrills she got out of it for a while. Then one day she woke up to the realization that she had fallen into the clutches of something, and she wanted out. But she didn't want to break free to come under God's control. And she told me that thousands of other young people have, almost innocently perhaps, gone down the road into the occult, looking for that middle ground where they can be in charge of themselves, independent of both God and Satan. She finally had to conclude, "I looked and looked for that little square inch, that little box between Satan and God, and I never found it. I finally decided I had better go under God's control, because that middle point didn't exist at all."

The same devil control had happened to the demoniac, but in the presence of Jesus, hope still existed for him. "None have fallen so low, none are so vile, but that they can find deliverance in Christ. The demoniac, in place of prayer, could utter only the words of Satan. Yet the heart's unspoken appeal was heard. No cry from a soul in need, though it fail of utterance in words, will be unheeded" (*ibid.*, p. 258).

Isn't it fantastic that although the man came into the temple blaspheming God, yet Jesus could look down into his heart and realize what he was trying to say? And even today the person who curses God has hope, for God can look down into his heart and realize that he might *really* be saying, "Help me, Lord. I need help!" Isn't it wonderful that the Holy Spirit translates our prayers and sometimes even our cursings into the cries for help that we're really trying to get across?

The man received release because Jesus came and set the captives free. He had earlier thought that he could play around with sin, going downhill until someday in the future, in a moment of extremity, he could turn around and head back. But he found himself under the bondage of another power, and he discovered too late that he was in the clutches of a someone that wouldn't free him, in the stranglehold of a force he couldn't break. Only the mighty power of God could liberate him and in the same process place him under His control. God could now rule over him.

And here the pride of the human heart begins to get nervous, for it resists anyone's, including God's, ruling instead of self. But "God does not control our minds without our consent" (ibid.). If you can accept that sentence, you can also reverse it and find that God does govern our minds with our permission.

"Wait!" comes the objection. "Don't do away with the dignity of man. Don't make puppets out of us. Remember, we're made in the image of God."

We have already shown that the false dignity of man has no place in the plan of salvation. And further, God's control is not the same as puppetry, because a puppet is always a puppet. It cannot be anything else. But a man, under God, always has the option to choose which power will rule over him. This still preserves the dignity of man and man's creation in the image of God. If we do not choose to accept God's leadership, we automatically fall under the control of Satan, even though we may not manifest extreme behavior as did the demoniac.

Does this mean that the Laodicean who sits in church each week, the good moral behaviorist who is trying to earn merit, substituting his actions in place of fellowship with Christ each day, is under the domination of Satan?

Yes. That's right. There is no middle ground. "The one who depends upon his own wisdom and power is separating himself from God. Instead of working in unison with Christ, he is fulfilling the purpose of the enemy of God and man" (ibid., p. 209).

"We must inevitably be under the control of the one or the other of the two great powers that are contending for the supremacy of the world. It is not necessary for us deliberately to choose the service of the kingdom of darkness in order to come under its dominion. We have only to neglect to ally ourselves with the kingdom of light. If we do not co-operate with the heavenly agencies, Satan will take possession of the heart, and will make it his abiding place" (*ibid.*, p. 324).

"Every soul that refuses to give himself to God is under the control of another power. He is not his own. He may talk of freedom, but he is in the most abject slavery. . . . His mind is under the control of Satan. While he flatters himself that he is following the dictates of his own judgment, he obeys the will of the prince of darkness" (*ibid.*, p. 466).

Jesus described this situation when He said, "He that is not with me is against me" (Matthew 12:30), for "no man can serve two masters" (Matthew 6:24). If you do not know Jesus as your personal friend, you are against Him. You may do good deeds and others may consider you a saintly Christian, but if you knowingly rely on your morality for salvation, you're lost.

I'd like to close this chapter with the premise and conclusion that it is our choice to respond to which power is going to rule over us, and that is all we can do. If the concept makes me nervous, it's simply the rebellion of my pride and ego, the instinctive reaction to brace my feet and resist the drawing power of God. And if I'm afraid I'll lose my freedom, then I should keep studying the nature of God's control until I understand what it includes and what it doesn't.

Rather than ending on the depressing note of condemnation of man's inherent nature and inabilities, I would like to remind you that God has provided a way out for us. He hasn't left us to serve Him as best we can under our handicapped condition. Nor does He make unreasonable, impossible demands without a solution.

Today I'm thankful for our Lord Jesus Christ who stood

up one day in the synagogue at Nazareth and announced His mission: "The Spirit of the Lord is upon me, because he hath anointed me to preach the gospel to the poor; he hath sent me to heal the brokenhearted, *to preach deliverance to the captives,* and recovering of sight to the blind, *to set at liberty* them that are bruised" (Luke 4:18).

Remember that Jesus delivered captives *in church* two thousand years ago. He cast out devils in the synagogue, not just in the gutter. And He's able and willing to do the same for you and me today. If I'm not presently under the control of God, if I haven't learned to surrender totally to Him, then I'm under the control of the evil one. But Jesus has the power to set me free, and He'll do it if I'll ask Him. He's the deliverer, and that's His mission. I'm thankful that I can be set free, that I can know what deliverance by God's grace from the captivity of sin means. And in this process which *God* does, I can enjoy the greatest freedom possible in the universe.

Chapter 3

The Freedom of Love

Does *God* work in us to will and do His good pleasure, or does God work in *us* to will and do? Is obedience in the Christian life natural or forced? Do I compel myself to be a good husband, or does it come naturally? If I have to force it, does it mean that I am not a good one? And if I have to make myself conform in the Christian life, does it mean that I don't really have what God intends for me? These are some of the practical questions that we are studying on the subject of the will.

In the last chapter we learned that we can do some things apart from a relationship with God. That when the power of God keeps us alive, we can do many things *externally*. But when it comes to cleansing or renewing the *inward* life, all of us are in the same boat. We can accomplish nothing. Since all are sinners, none can change the heart or deeper springs of action. Jesus refers to the inward life when He says that without Him (or without a relationship with Him), we "can do nothing" (John 15:5).

We also notice that Jesus said, "He that is not with me is against me" (Matthew 12:30). I don't have to oppose or mistreat my wife to be against her. If I'm not for her, I'm against her. Remember that "in the great conflict for the soul of man, there is no middle ground; neutrality is impossible. . . . Every man is either a patriot or a traitor. He who is not

wholly on the side of Christ is wholly on the side of the
enemy. . . . To be almost, but not wholly, with Christ is to be,
not almost, but wholly against Him" (*SDA Bible Commentary,*
Vol. 5, p. 395).

Inevitably we stand under the control of one or the other of
two great powers. No third option exists. We don't have the
choice of being under God, under Satan, or under the control
of ourselves and our own brilliant minds. It is either one or the
other of the two great powers. Either the wicked one or Christ
dominates us. Some people become nervous over that fact.
"We're looking for liberty. Doesn't the Bible talk about
freedom? Are you saying that if we leave Satan, we can be only
under God?" Yes. "Then where does freedom come in, in the
Christian life?"

In order to accept the control of God willingly, we have to
understand more about the *type* of guidance that God places
on us. What makes domination by Christ legitimate? How can
surrendering ourselves to come under His rulership still be
acceptable, palatable, and desirable? How can surrender to
God's control bring us freedom?

Jesus declared, "The Spirit of the Lord is upon me, because
he hath anointed me . . . to preach deliverance to the captives,
. . . to set at liberty them that are bruised" (Luke 4:18). Then
how can He "free" us by controlling us without placing us
under duress and undesirable force?

First of all, we have a clue in Romans 8:2, where Paul
suggests that "the law of the Spirit of life in Christ Jesus hath
made me free from the law of sin and death." So a life in Christ
carries freedom that one of sin and death does not. How does
He accomplish it? "The Lord hath appeared of old unto me,
saying, Yea, I have loved thee with an everlasting love:
therefore with lovingkindness have I drawn thee" (Jeremiah
31:3). Jesus uses the power of love. "Lovingkindness" makes
the difference between unwanted domination by the evil one

and the longed-for freedom that comes through Christ's control.

If you have a happy marriage, you will have no problem at all in understanding this. When in love, you will do things for your companion that you would never do under any other circumstances, things that you would never do for your neighbor. What makes the difference? Love—the greatest force in the world. Nothing equals it. Talk about the force of arms—why, Napoleon couldn't even come close. And he finally admitted it at his banishment: "Alexander, Caesar, Charlemagne, and I have founded empires. But on what did we rest the creations of our genius? Upon force. Jesus Christ founded his empire upon love; and at this hour millions of men would die for him." Generals could not really conquer with the force of arms. Love conquers, and it brings freedom.

Someone suggested the analogy of the two great powers in the world. America has been known as the land of the free. If I am a citizen of America, I am free. I live in the "free world," not in a totalitarian state. But when Uncle Sam says, "I need you; I want you," I am a slave because I am a citizen. And thousands of GIs in our past wars—when they heard the general give the order—have gone "over the top" amid a rain of bullets. As MacArthur said, "The American soldier is magnificent. He wades through the mud and the sleet and the blood and the snow. He moans, he groans, he curses, and he dies. Magnificent!" Why does he do it? Why did hundreds of thousands of them do it? Because they were citizens of a free country. They were also slaves.

Well, suppose I am a citizen of another country not considered part of the "free world." I am still a citizen, but I am not free. In fact, I am a slave, even without war. What makes the difference? Do I love my country, or am I involved in a system of duress or force? Would I throw it off in a moment if I had a chance? Would I rather be a man without a country? How does this apply to our relationship with God?

When a person breaks from the tyranny of the evil one, which he can do only through the power of God, then freedom begins. "In the change that takes place when the soul surrenders to Christ, there is the highest sense of freedom. . . . The only condition upon which the freedom of man is possible is that of becoming one with Christ" (*The Desire of Ages*, p. 466).

The people in the days of Christ didn't feel a need for this freedom. Jesus said to them one day, "If the Son therefore shall make you free, ye shall be free indeed" (John 8:36). They replied, "Who is a slave? We were never in bondage to anyone." The same spirit actuated those who felt abhorrence in the presence of the demoniac in Capernaum as had motivated the demoniac himself. The devil controlled them just as much as he did the insane man (*ibid.*, p. 256). Can it happen today? Do I struggle for a sense of freedom which I do not now possess? Do you? Is your experience in living the Christian life simply a burden and a constant load on your shoulders? Are you frustrating yourself in trying to conform, trying to live up to certain expectations that are way beyond you?

Watchman Nee in his book *Not I, But Christ* (New York: Christian Fellowship Publishers, Inc., 1974) has said it rather emphatically but truly nonetheless. It sounds shocking at first, and I am going to presume to quote excerpts from one chapter. See if it fits your case in any sense concerning the break from slavery to the search for freedom. He says that the way to freedom lies in the substitutionary life of Christ—that Christ became our substitute, not only dying in our place, but living in our place.

"At the beginning of our Christian life, we saw how the Lord Jesus bore our sins on the cross so that by His death we were delivered from death, our sins were forgiven, and we were condemned no more. Today Paul tells me that because Christ lives in me, I am delivered from living" (pp. 110, 111).

It sounds strange to say that I am delivered from living. Haven't we always heard that we are to live for Christ? He explains that "since He lives in me, I no longer need to live. As He died on the cross for me, so now He lives in me in my place. This is the secret of victory. This is Paul's secret. He does not say, 'I hope I will not need to live,' or, 'I hope I can let Him live.' He just says, 'No longer live I, for I have let Him live. Now it is no longer I who live, but Christ who lives in me.'

"Let us pray much that God will enlighten us to see that man has no need to live for himself because Christ can live in him. The day that you heard you did not need to die, you felt this was a great gospel. Now, in another day, you are hearing that you do not need to live. This is also a great gospel" (ibid., p. 111).

"Many try to resist sin, but do not have the strength. Yet, if they do not resist, they will not have inward peace. Many want to be patient but cannot. When they lose their temper, they feel uneasy in their hearts. They have no heart strength to love; but if they hate, their hearts condemn them. They really feel it is a heavy burden to be a Christian. It gives them a sensation of climbing uphill with a heavy load. Many people will tell you that before they believed in the Lord Jesus, they were heavily laden with the load of sin; now, having believed, they are heavily laden with the burden of holiness. It is only substituting one burden for another; both are tiresome and heavy" (ibid., pp. 111, 112).

Who said, "Come unto me, . . . and I will give you rest"? Was He referring only to rest from subjection to the evil one? Or was He also talking about the rest that comes from freedom in being controlled by God? Is the burden of holiness any lighter than that of sin? The author goes on to explain, "If this

situation described above is the case, it certainly means that
these Christians have been misinstructed. It is wrong for a
person to attempt to live the Christian life. We are not asked to
do so. The Word of the Lord says, 'It is no longer I that live, but
Christ liveth in me.' This is the secret of Christian living. The
Lord in me lives the Christian life, not I. If I have been trying
to live like a Christian, in patience, love, kindness, humility,
sorrow or cross-bearing, it is rather painful. But if it is Christ
who lives in me, in patience, love, suffering, or cross-bearing,
it is joyful" (*ibid.*, p. 112).

It sounds exaggerated. Some old-guard Christians would
immediately throw the book in the flames. But wait a minute.
Think about it. It's simply stating what Jesus and Paul were
trying to say. We obey *in Christ*, not because we try hard to
obey, but because we would have to struggle *not* to. In other
words, obedience in the Christian life is natural for the one
who has the loving relationship of trust in the Lord Jesus.

So when someone says, "I haven't lost my temper for three
years, but I haven't wanted to for three days," does he have
spiritual victory, or has he been sitting on a lid of conformity,
trying to rein himself back to keep from doing what he really
wants to do? If I am forcing myself to refrain from doing
certain things simply because someone told me that I mustn't
do them, have I really overcome anything? A legalist who
relies on outward behavior for salvation would say that I have,
but God has a better plan—to give me freedom also from the
desire to do wrong. If I go around giving people the impression that living a Christian life consists of trying hard to obey,
am I truly representing God's plan? Or am I simply advertis-
ing the fact that I am an immature Christian who hasn't
understood God's great plan of salvation by faith yet?

Now, to avoid any misunderstanding I would like to
describe natural obedience. I am not talking about the person
who sits in his rocking chair all day and lets Christ work his

job and make his living for him. Christ does not bypass us—He lives *in us*. Paul said, "It is no longer I who live, but Christ who lives *in me*" (Galatians 2:20, RSV).

Perhaps I can explain better by an illustration. When my brother attended La Sierra College, he fell in love and planned to get married when school ended. So one cold, dark Saturday night, with pea-soup fog all around, he started out for Glendale to see his fiancée. He had no way to get the seventy-five miles into Glendale that night from La Sierra, but he wanted to visit her. So he started walking. My brother had definitely fallen in love. The students at our end of the dormitory knew that he was in love. Nobody thought that he had lost his mind because he was walking in the dark to Glendale. Everybody assumed it was the most natural thing for him to do. His feet went down the road, and his thumb stuck out, trying to catch a ride through the pea-soup fog when the motorists couldn't even see his thumb. He expended tremendous energy to make it to Glendale. But love controlled him, urged him on. It would have been unnatural for him to stay at home with his feet on the desk, reading a book. In other words, even though he had to put forth effort, it was the *natural* result of love. It was his choice—what he really wanted to do. *Love* was stronger than the hassle of walking through the fog in the dark.

When we talk about natural obedience in the Christian life, this is what we mean. It is not effortless, but it is natural. No other force in the world compares to it. The drive that comes from love carries freedom with it because love makes a person *desire* to obey. He no longer feels he *has* to because of fear. Instead he *wants* to because of love. The love of Christ motivates us to do things that would have been against our nature before. So if I am living the Christian life by forcing myself to obey and have been sitting on a lid ready to blow for years, there's something wrong.

I'd like to suggest several major reasons why obedience in the Christian life must be and is natural.

1. First of all, as we noticed in the last chapter, because of man's inherent sinful nature, he is incapable of any real goodness apart from faith in the power of God and a vital connection with Him.

Trolley cars still run in some of our larger cities. At the top of the cars a pole travels along the power line. Whenever something separates the car from the wire, it can no longer run. If I were the conductor of a stalled trolley car, I could use my effort in two ways. I could work to restore the connection between the car and the power, or I could get behind the trolley and start pushing. To do the latter would misuse my ability to choose, for all my shoving would not start the car again. But if I decide to restore the connection with the power source, then the trolley car would go naturally.

And we're like those trolley cars that can operate only when in touch with the overhead power, for the moment their connection breaks, they cease to move. In the Christian life we cannot grow without our union with God. Our allowing God to dominate our lives through the power of love is a constant necessity. Any moment that we separate ourselves from dependence on Christ we have the same clamors of the evil heart with which we were born, mainly of selfishness. We can never partially surrender, because when God does a job, He does it totally and completely (Philippians 1:6). We are either totally surrendered to Christ at any given moment or totally dependent on our own power. If we rely upon God, then our obedience will be a spontaneous result (*Steps to Christ*, p. 60; *Christ's Object Lessons*, pp. 97, 98).

2. Obedience is natural because fruits in the Christian life, as in the orchard, are the normal, automatic outgrowth. And fruits of the Spirit include the obedience of love and of faith (Galatians 5:22, 23).

By the way, do you know that the two greatest needs of the church of God are faith and love? They are both fruits of the Spirit, but the Spirit Himself is a gift (1 Corinthians 12:1, 7). Sometime make a list of the things that come as gifts in the Christian life. You'll find that faith (Ephesians 2:8), righteousness (Romans 5:17), victory (1 Corinthians 15:57), grace (1 Peter 5:5), peace (John 14:27), glory (John 17:22), eternal life (John 3:16; 1 John 2:25), white robes (Revelation 3:5), Jesus (John 3:16), the water of life (Revelation 21:6), the crown of life (Revelation 2:10), the bread of life (John 6:26-35, 51), conversion (John 3), repentance (Acts 5:31), and love (1 John 3:1; 4:7; 2 Timothy 1:7)—all are gifts. And no one can receive *anything* unless God gives it to him (John 3:27). No wonder Jesus said, "To whom much is given, of him will much be required" (Luke 12:48, RSV). We have a whole tree full of gifts, including every necessity in the Christian life.

3. You don't have to work for something that is a gift. You have only to come into relationship with the person who offers it, and he'll present it to you. Then obedience in the Christian life would naturally follow.

4. Obedience in living the Christian life is also natural because of love. Love motivates us (2 Corinthians 5:14). My brother's love for his fiancée impelled him to walk to Glendale to see her. *Love* controls.

God's plan is to control us, but never against our choice or our will. That's why He is so diametrically opposed to hypnotism. "It is not God's purpose that any human being should yield his mind and will to the control of another, becoming a passive instrument in his hands. No one is to merge his individuality in that of another. He is not to look to any human being. . . . His dependence must be in God. In the *dignity* of his God-given manhood he is to be *controlled by God Himself,* not by any human intelligence" (*The Ministry of Healing,* p. 242, italics supplied).

Can a person still maintain the dignity of creation in the image of God while being controlled by God? That's what it says. Why is God so opposed to hypnotism? Because in it a person makes a choice to place himself under the control of mere man, and that puts man on the same level with God.

Let's just follow it through. The theory in hypnotism is that I choose to place myself under the authority of another, who then makes the choices for me, through me. The force of love is missing. And the hypnotism becomes a perfect example of the control that Satan exerts, because it contains no freedom. Once I'm in a trance, I cannot break free until or unless the hypnotist chooses to bring me out of it. The same thing happens in Satan's kingdom. I'm stuck with control—the plight of the man in the synagogue at Capernaum. A power that wouldn't let go held him. Even if he chose to be free, he couldn't liberate himself. But Jesus heard his cry for help and released him.

Let's paraphrase the statement on hypnotism by turning it around to the positive side, the way God invites us to live: It *is* God's purpose that every human being should yield his mind and will to the control of God. We've sung all our lives, "Have Thine own way, Lord! Have Thine own way! Thou art the Potter; I am the clay." Sounds nice in song, doesn't it? But do we really mean it? It's the word *passive* that bothers us. But don't forget how *active* "passive" can be. "[It is God's purpose that every human being should yield his mind and will to the control of God and become a passive instrument in God's hands]. . . . He is not to look to any human being. . . . His dependence must be in God. In the *dignity* of his God-given manhood he is to be controlled by God Himself."

Now I wasn't paraphrasing the last part. God Himself is to control me. But I don't have to be nervous, because love makes the whole plan legitimate, free, and beautiful. I can trust God to preserve my dignity, my individuality, and my personality.

If I was a "stubborn Dutchman" before conversion, will God change my individuality? No. I'll still be stubborn, but rather than for myself I'll be determined for God and His cause. What makes the difference? Love. And it's different from hypnotism, because when I choose to let God control me, I'm always free at any given moment to not allow Him to guide my life any longer. I can decide to leave and submit to Satan's power if I desire to. But I don't want to—I've had enough of that. I prefer the freedom that comes with the control of love.

5. Jesus gave us an example in living natural obedience when He let His Father direct His life (John 14:10), and we'll discuss it in detail in a later chapter. God even made His plans for Him (*The Ministry of Healing*, p. 479; *The Desire of Ages*, p. 208). And in John 14:10, RSV, Christ stated, "The Father who dwells in me does his works." Jesus was essentially saying, "It is no longer I who live, but My Father who lives in Me." How? Through some kind of dangerous domination? No. By His own choice, made at the beginning of every day, by a relationship of love. If we had the slightest idea of the closeness of the love of God and His Son, we would be amazed. Jesus' heart was finally broken on the cross because He *felt* His Father had forsaken Him (Matthew 27:46; *The Desire of Ages*, p. 753; *Testimonies for the Church*, Vol. 2, p. 210).

6. Natural obedience is also God's intent for us in the Christian life, because of the example of our initial conversion experience. He invites us to walk in Christ's footsteps *in the same way* in which we first became Christians (Colossians 2:6). There's no difference between living the Christian life and becoming a Christian. In becoming one I could do nothing except to come to Christ. That was all I could do then, and that's all I can do now in remaining one.

7. The final reason for natural obedience is the argument of faith and works. Should you have studied it at all, you

know that faith in Christ is completely the *cause* of our Christianity and salvation, while works of obedience are totally the
result. If the premise of righteousness by faith is true, then
obedience in the Christian life has to be natural.

But what kind of freedom does it bring? Many kinds. It
frees me to be myself, instead of trying to fake it and pretend
I'm something that I'm not. If I do not know what it means to
be in a surrendered relationship to Jesus Christ, even though I
am a member of the Christian church, I am faking it twenty-
four hours a day. I'm playing the role, and that's slavery. No
wonder young people break away from it! But when the
motivation of love has awakened the response in my heart and
I love because He first loved me, I don't have to pretend any
longer. I can be myself, for God's control doesn't destroy my
will or my personality.

Now I have another freedom that I never could have had
before. I can say no to God at any time, but I can do it in two
ways. As I am experiencing a daily, meaningful relationship
with God, I could come to the point where I can declare, "No
thanks, I don't want it any longer. I don't want to be under
Your control any more." Also at those moments of decision
involving specific problems and temptations, I could state,
"No thanks, I don't want to listen to the Holy Spirit on this
particular point. I'll do my own thing." Therefore I have two
freedoms: I can break the daily relationship, or I can choose to
take over and depend on myself on any given point. God's
purpose for me as a growing Christian is to teach me constant
dependence on Him in all things and at all times. Sometimes
I'll learn only through hard knocks. But the freedom comes
through God's control, and with it come joy and peace in
listening to His invitation on every point and every decision.

I also have freedom in another area: Neither man nor the
devil can manipulate me. A classic example appears in Paul's
life. As a result of witnessing for God, he received beatings,

stonings, and imprisonment. Finally, alone in a dungeon cell, he wrote, "I have learned, in whatsoever state I am, therewith to be content" (Philippians 4:11). Paul had learned not to let situations, circumstances, or the actions of others around him dictate the way he felt or acted. His security was in God alone. He was God-sufficient.

When I'm free in Christ, people can no longer maneuver my actions. I no longer have to worry about the pressures of conformity. And if someone acts hostile to me, I don't have to react according to the way he treats me. *People* can't hurt me or my feelings.

Since my security no longer lies in my power to manipulate or tear them down, I am also free from manipulating others. My relationship with the Lord Jesus forms the basis of my security.

I am free to love other people without needing them to love me back. No longer do I have to keep score of the good deeds done to me before I return them. Wouldn't it be terrible to be a slave to sending out Christmas presents and taking inventory after Christmas Eve to make sure I get as much back as I gave? Wouldn't it be too bad to love only those who love me? Isn't that the crippling dilemma of the unrenewed heart? That type of love is cheap and synthetic. It restricts me, for I am free only to love those who already love me. But Jesus loved a world that did not love Him. He still continues to love the unlovable.

I find the freedom to forgive, because God has forgiven me. And what I forgive, though little in proportion to the amount I have been forgiven, is now easy because of Christ's love. Now I don't have to keep poisoning my mind with grudges that I hold against those who have done me wrong. My mind is free from hatred, resentment, and a desire for revenge.

The freedoms that I can know in Christ are endless and

infinite. I don't have to play God by trying to save myself and then seeing myself fail again and again. Christ removes the worry about getting in all my living just on earth—I can live forever. And my eternal life isn't a future promise. It is a reality that begins as soon as I enter into relationship with God (*The Desire of Ages*, p. 388; John 17:3).

How can I experience the control of love? Is it through some sort of self-induced mind manipulation in which I decide once and for all that from now on I want to be under God's control? No. The only thing I can do is to admit at the beginning of each day that I am not sufficient, that life is too big for me. And then I can go to my knees for that thoughtful hour in contemplation of Christ's life. All I need to do is to make the choice each day to stay in the devotional relationship where the love is (1 Corinthians 13:4-7). My daily growth in that relationship constitutes what we call sanctification. Jesus fulfills His promise to bring deliverance. The highest sense of freedom results from being under His control. God's domination, always by my choice, is given with love, and that takes the danger away.

Love alone can make and keep me steadfast. It "alone can enable . . . [us] to withstand trial and temptation" (*Christ's Object Lessons*, p. 49). Please accept the invitation of Jesus to remain free from the dictatorship of the powers of this world and to enter into the liberty and freedom that come from willing submission to God's love.

Chapter 4

Being Good by Not Being Bad

In studying the role that a human being plays in living the Christian life, we have already discovered that the *obedience* of faith is the natural product of a valid Christian experience. Saving faith, however, is in a certain sense deliberated; that is, we consciously choose it by seeking the daily relationship with Jesus Christ. The *results* of that saving faith—doing what's right, living a good life (inwardly as well as outwardly)—are not coerced. Whenever I have to force myself to obey by trying to conform to the principles of conduct in Christian life, I am simply acknowledging that I'm an immature Christian.

This concept would sound dangerously like "rocking-chair" religion or "easy-going" faith were it not for the fact that we must do one thing ourselves, do it deliberately—come to Christ, seek God daily to know Him personally. He cannot do it for us, because He has granted us freedom of choice. While He'll use His Spirit, the angels, and the entire forces of heaven to draw us, we must make the choice to respond by seeking Him and allowing Him to control our lives. "The Lord can do nothing toward the recovery of man until, convinced of his own weakness, and stripped of all self-sufficiency, *he yields himself to the control of God.* Then he can receive the gift that God is waiting to bestow. From the soul that feels his need, nothing is withheld. He has

unrestricted access to Him in whom all fullness dwells"
(*The Desire of Ages,* p. 300, italics supplied).

Now, someone is sure to ask if it is wrong to be "good"
if he doesn't really feel like it. Many young people have
raised the question. "Theoretically we understand the
concept of salvation and relationship through faith in
Christ," they explain. "But if we've been forcing ourselves
to do what's right, then for the sake of salvation through
faith in Christ alone, hadn't we better stop being good so
that 'grace may abound' in our lives? What are we
supposed to do while our faith is growing to the ideal point
of constant natural obedience? If we try hard to keep
obeying deliberately, will that ruin everything? Or if we
feel like committing fornication or adultery, would it be
just as well to go ahead, then?"

Although being good by not being externally bad is not
being good, as far as God is concerned, there's no question
that man considers it as good. If I feel like killing someone,
but manage to restrain myself from doing it, I will have
some real benefits. I'll keep out of jail, and I won't have the
guilt of a murder on my hands. (But I'll probably give
myself credit for having enough willpower to control my
actions.) Certainly morality has all kinds of advantages as
far as man and the law view it. But external goodness
contains no real righteousness as far as God is concerned.
In fact, it can even make one feel secure apart from God.

I'd like to illustrate my premise by reminding you of the
plight of Laodicea: "I know thy works, that thou art neither
cold nor hot: *I would thou wert cold or hot.* So then because
thou art lukewarm, and neither cold nor hot, I will spue
thee out of my mouth. . . . Thou sayest, I am rich, and
increased with goods, and have need of nothing; and
knowest not that thou art wretched, and miserable, and
poor, and blind, and naked" (Revelation 3:15-17).

Laodicea's biggest problem is its self-sufficiency and resulting external goodness. It is known for its morality, but not for its genuine righteousness or for its faith. Therefore the goodness of Laodicea is forced, and God tells them what He thinks about their calculated goodness—He wishes they were either hot or cold. He considers external goodness worthless in terms of salvation and sanctification. Further, He declares that He is going to reject those who are only externally good, for He has no place for them. They must go one way or the other.

Another scripture, Matthew 23, describes the goodness of the Pharisees in Christ's day. Apparently their condition was the same as in Laodicea, and it has been a lasting problem, the great danger of depending upon our morality or external ethics to commend us to God. "Woe unto you, scribes and Pharisees, hypocrites! for ye compass sea and land to make one proselyte, and when he is made, ye make him twofold more the child of hell than yourselves" (verse 15). Christ declared that those who campaign for others to be externally good as they are themselves will only make them twofold worse off than themselves.

Steps to Christ uses even plainer language and perhaps more modern vernacular. "There are those who profess to serve God, while they rely upon their own efforts to obey His law, to form a right character, and secure salvation. Their hearts are not moved by any deep sense of the love of Christ, but they seek to perform the duties of the Christian life as that which God requires of them in order to gain heaven. *Such religion is worth nothing*" (p. 44, italics supplied).

I would also like to remind you of Webster's definition of morality and of the comment we have already quoted from *Christ's Object Lessons:* "Many who call themselves Christians are mere human moralists" (p. 315). The same writer has also said that "none are living Christians unless they have a daily experience in the things of God" (*Testimonies for the Church*, Vol. 2, p. 505). And, by the way, "things of God" refers to that which has to do with seeking God in the personal, daily, one-to-one relationship, acquaintance, fellowship, and communion with Him.

"Wait a minute!" someone objects. "Isn't morality worth something? Maybe it will lead me to God eventually." The apostle Paul said, "By the deeds of the law there shall no flesh be justified: . . . for by the law is the knowledge of sin" (Romans 3:20). Our good works will not bring us to God. The law only shows us our sins so that we will seek God. In fact, he warned that a person who tries to accomplish righteousness by his own efforts will end up in the worst trap of all—pride in his external goodness (Romans 9:30-33; 10:1-4). Remember, the gospel has no room for boasting or human pride. "Where is boasting then? It is excluded. By what law? of works? Nay: but by the law of faith. Therefore we conclude that a man is justified by faith without the deeds of the law" (Romans 3:27, 28).

According to the Biblical record and Jesus' own statements, God's plan of salvation has no room for simply being externally good apart from Christ through not being bad. It has never been His plan, and it never will be. The only legitimate obedience in the Christian life comes as a spontaneous result of our relationship with Christ.

If being good by not being bad were our method, then we would be operating our wills in the wrong way. God never intended us to employ them toward being good. He wanted us to use them only toward knowing Him. "*All true* obedience comes from the heart. It was heart work with Christ. And if we consent, He will so identify Himself with our thoughts and aims, so blend our hearts and minds into conformity to His will, that when obeying Him we shall be but carrying out our own impulses. The will, refined and sanctified, will find its highest delight in doing His service. *When we know God as it is our privilege to know Him,* our life will be a life of continual obedience. Through an appreciation of the character of Christ, *through communion with God,* sin will become hateful to us" (*The Desire of Ages,* p. 668, italics supplied). In other words, we are to direct our power of choice *totally* toward knowing Him in a daily, personal relationship. And in doing so, we give up our power of choice that we ordinarily exercise toward *things,* toward being good by ourselves, or toward restraining ourselves from being bad.

"But," you say, "won't this lead to license?" No! Contrary to teaching license and immorality, righteousness through faith in Christ alone is the only thing that allows for anything other than license and immorality, because righteousness by faith in Jesus is the only kind of real righteousness there is.

So in the Christian experience of salvation by faith alone, we are to channel our power of choice and our willpower toward the continuing relationship of knowing God rather than directing it toward behavior. We can safely do so because when we choose the relationship, then *God* works in us to will (choose) and to do (behave). It doesn't mean that we cannot take our choice and our willpower back at any time. Haven't you noticed, however, that if you've experienced enough of the folly of relying on yourself and your own decisions, you don't want to ask for your power of choice back? Have you ever gone astray so much and so often in using your will and willpower on your own that you didn't want to employ it that way any more?

I'd like to give you a simple example. In 1958 I needed a new car, and a local church friend who ran a used-car lot told me about a Cadillac he had there. It was only five years old and had sat in a garage for two years. You know the story: "Little old lady from Pasadena who used it just to go to the store." And it cost half the price of a brand-new Chevrolet. Well, the truth is, I had always wanted a Cadillac. (And it wasn't the status of owning a Cadillac, either, I'm sure—or so I told myself. I just liked the way the thing ran. All I had to do was step on the gas, and it sort of glided along quietly—I couldn't even hear the engine.) My wife opposed buying it from the start, but after a great deal of talking along the lines of "they never wear out, they never depreciate; the engines just get better the older they are; they get more gas mileage than a Chevy," and all the rest of it, I had my Cadillac. I was proud of it, and it soon became my idol. Soon I discovered, though, that my church members had other ideas, for they began ribbing me about it until when I'd go to visit somebody, I'd drive down three blocks and over two and then walk back five so they wouldn't see the car.

One day, not long after I got it, the radiator overheated on the way to San Francisco. Apparently it *had* rested in the garage for two years. It was rusty and caused the head on the engine to crack. The next morning, when I tried to start my car, it acted like the battery was dead. I didn't know that a cylinder was full of water and was locking tightly; so I had my neighbor push the car to start it. Then the transmission went out. Now I had a ruined engine and transmission, and when the rear end went out as well, I decided it was a judgment from God. The truth is that it was the result of my own willing and doing apart from Him. After getting the engine repaired and the transmission and the rear end and everything else fixed up (including new wall-to-wall carpet, because I found it was rotten underneath), it was like a new car. But I was never so happy to get rid of anything (for a loss) in my life.

When I bought that car, I knew that I was not asking God for guidance. I didn't *want* it, for I was afraid He would say no. Instead, I deliberately went ahead and bought it under the realization that I was living apart from God concerning that choice. I wanted to make my own decision. And I've had just enough of those kinds of experiences to know that when I am willful and doing it on my own, I often really ruin it. Even if I should happen to make the right choice for a change, I discover that I don't have the power to do it. If I had willed, apart from God, not to buy that Cadillac, I probably would have bought it just the same.

So in our surrender of the will to God we are not kissing it good-bye forever. We can take it back at any moment, can choose another master. But if we've had enough of the experiences that go with living life apart from God, we won't want it back.

In the first chapter I alluded to a description in *Steps to Christ*, page 47, of the surrender of the will, and now I'd like to cite the whole difficult paragraph that starts out with great hopes and ends up in apparent confusion: "Many are inquiring, '*How* am I to make the surrender of myself to God?' You desire to give yourself to Him, but you are weak in moral power, in slavery to doubt, and controlled by the habits of your life of sin. Your promises and resolutions are like ropes of sand. You cannot control your thoughts, your impulses, your affections. The knowledge of your broken promises and forfeited pledges weakens your confidence in your own sincerity, and causes you to feel that God cannot accept you; but you need not despair."

When I first read that, I could understand the problem it portrayed. It described me—my condition. And it gave me a gleam of courage—"you need not despair"! The answer seemed forthcoming. But when I tried to read *it*, I couldn't understand it. And that's where I began the game of skipping that part and trying to forget that page. Finally one day, in desperation, I sat down and began to read the page slowly. "What you need to understand is the true force of the will" *(ibid.)*.

The same paragraph defines the will as "the governing power in the nature of man, the power of decision, or of choice." Then the will is the power of decision or choice, and willpower, which we've often confused with the will, is the power *to do* what we've chosen to do. Will is the power to choose, and willpower is the ability to put our decision into effect. In Philippians 2:13 God promises to *both will* (choose) and to *do* in us. If we replace the definition of the will (power of choice) wherever the word *will* shows up in this *Steps to Christ* paragraph, then it reads, "Everything depends on the right action of the . . . [*power of choice*]. The power of choice God has given to men; it is theirs to exercise. You cannot change your heart, you cannot of yourself give to God its affections; but you can *choose* to serve Him" *(ibid.)*.

What does the paragraph mean? First of all, it indicates that there exists a right and a wrong action of the will. (The right action is seeking God; the wrong is trying to be good through my own power.) It also says that I cannot change my sinful nature, even though I can alter my outward actions to conform to certain standards. Notice the last phrase: "but you can *choose* to serve Him." It doesn't say that you can choose to do what's right. It isn't choosing *what to do*—it's *whom to serve*. And the word *serve* suggests servitude, being a servant. He is our master, we are His servants. Submission, surrender. Then it states that we can give Him our will, *or* we can give Him our power of choice.

But someone begins to get nervous. What about the dignity of man? The dignity of man remains preserved as long as he has the continuing ability to decide whether or not to give his power of choice, because as long as he has that ability, he can never be a slave, an automaton, or a machine.

And what happens when you give God your power of choice? "He will then work in you to will and to do according to His good pleasure. Thus your whole nature will be brought under the *control* of the Spirit of Christ; your affections will be centered upon Him, your thoughts will be in harmony with Him" (*ibid.*, italics supplied).

Here the word *control* appears again. But remember that God's control is safe and legitimate because it originates in *love*. And when we're under God's guidance, our thoughts will be in harmony with His. Now the humanist, the self-sufficient man, the scholar, the achiever, the wealthy, and the mighty man may not like that. It offends them because it threatens their ego and pride. But the apostle Paul was probably one of the greatest of men, and he submitted to it willingly. Why not the rest of us?

The next page in *Steps to Christ* then portrays the results of our surrender of the will to Him. "Through the right exercise of the will, an entire change may be made in your life. By yielding up your will [power of choice] to Christ, you ally yourself with the power that is above all principalities and powers. You will have strength from above to hold you steadfast, and thus through constant surrender to God you will be enabled to live the new life, even the life of faith." It merely says that God chooses, then does His will in me when I surrender. Paul describes it thus: "It is no longer I who live, but Christ who lives in me" (Galatians 2:20, RSV).

In case you are becoming nervous about God's eliminating the will, I'd like to assure you that He never abolishes it. "God does not design that our will should be destroyed, for it is only through its exercise that we can accomplish what He would have us do" (*Thoughts From the Mount of Blessing*, p. 62). In other words, I exercise my will to give it up to God. What happens next? "Our will is to be yielded to Him, that we may receive it again, purified and refined, and so linked in sympathy with the Divine that He can pour through us the tides of His love and power" *(ibid.)*.

Does Ellen White mean our will is an entity of itself that we can detach and take to the cleaners and then get back? No. When it comes back, it has God in *control* of it. Probably the closest description of what happens appears in *Christ's Object Lessons*, page 312: "When we submit ourselves to Christ, the heart is united with His heart, the will is merged in His will, the mind becomes one with His mind, the thoughts are brought into captivity to Him; we live His life. This is what it means to be clothed with the garment of His righteousness." Remember, I can choose to leave His control. His leadership is always by my choice, never by His pressure.

So God never takes away our will or our willpower. He only asks us, invites us, compels us *by love*, to use our will for choosing the ongoing relationship with Him while allowing Him to use our surrendered will toward everything else. Thus Paul can say in one place, "Work hard," and in another, "Don't work." The subject of the will or how to use our human effort in relation to divine power is then the pivot point in salvation by faith.

But here we again encounter the question, "Should we stop trying to do what's right, then? Is it wrong to force ourselves to behave properly?" People unfairly accused the apostle Paul, known as a preacher of righteousness by faith, of teaching this. "Not rather, (as we be slanderously reported . . .) Let us do evil, that good may come" (Romans 3:8). He answers by saying that those who charge him with promoting license deserve their own condemnation.

In verse 31 he asks, "Do we then make void the law through faith? God forbid: yea, we establish the law." Faith leaves us *more* obedient, not less. It alone can make it possible for Christ to keep the law in and through us.

In Romans 6:15, 16, Paul illustrates God's control in terms of captivity or slavery to a higher power. "What then? shall we sin, because we are not under the law, but under grace? God forbid. Know ye not, that to whom ye yield yourselves servants to obey, his servants ye are to whom ye obey; whether of sin unto death, or of obedience unto righteousness?"

It is unsafe to give young people the impression that they must stop trying to do what's right, if they don't know how to start trying to know Jesus. Why? Because the way we stop attempting to do what's right is by seeking to know Jesus.

But some may still object that others will stop struggling to do what's "right" now for the purpose of learning to know Jesus later, and thus open the door for an interim of anarchy. I'd like to propose that it is an unfounded fear because of an obvious conclusion: The strong person who has *succeeded* in behaving morally through his willpower and backbone without Christ will continue what's "right" for selfish reasons, whether or not he hears about salvation through faith in Christ. A person who has succeeded in staying out of trouble and out of jail will not suddenly scrap everything. I haven't seen a "strong" person yet who became immoral because he decided that righteousness by faith meant that he could go ahead and do whatever he had always wanted to do anyway so that "grace may abound."

Also I'd like to suggest that the weak person who hasn't succeeded in doing right is going to continue that way until he experiences genuine faith, and he won't be any worse off than he was before. The only one who fears that righteousness by faith will promote license is one who has some kind of belief that a weak person could do better if he would only try harder. And it's a false hope. Is the strong person fearful that another might stop trying to do good and become immoral?

Or, as someone suggested recently, the real problem could be that, realizing the weak individual might find an excuse or reason to continue in his present condition, the stronger one becomes jealous because he has always been weak inwardly himself and wishes he could be so outwardly, too, just for the fun of it. Is it possible that he objects to license for the weak because he wants it for himself? (See Luke 15:25-30.) His reaction proves, of course, his complete hypocrisy. Perhaps, too, the strong person finds in the pulling of the rug from underneath his morality such a blast to his pride that he cannot stand it.

It is an irrelevant, insignificant fear to think that allowing people to do what they really *want* to do *within the faith relationship* will cause license. *Love* is the safeguard against license. The experience of faith is the only thing that will change either the strong or the weak when it comes to cleansing their *inner* springs of action, and neither has an advantage here.

Then someone else inquires, "Doesn't God ever use righteousness by works to lead to righteousness by faith?" Has He ever done it? Do you think He does now? Somehow we've read quotes from Ellen G. White out of context and come up with the idea that parents should teach their children righteousness by habit, which will keep them out of jail long enough to enable them to find Christ when they're older. Haven't you heard the concept or variations of it? We've been eminently successful on this.

Let's face it—Laodicea has done a bang-up job here. And what have been the results? Are the young people able to understand righteousness through Jesus, faith, and surrender? No. It hasn't opened the door any wider for faith and experience with Christ. Often they can't even see Christ at all. Tired of being moral only externally, they leave the church. It galls them to discover themselves to be two different people—something different on the outside than they are on the inside.

Read in context the statements on training our children from the cradle on up in habits of proper behavior and you will discover that you can't separate such guidance from emphasis on the power, love, and grace of Jesus Christ. If you do, you destroy them. I have talked with young people completely incapable of fathoming what salvation through faith in Christ alone really means, because they are so steeped and brainwashed into their mold of morality and external goodness. Righteousness by faith sounds like some strange language to them. And as a result they apparently cannot understand the real relationship with God until they are almost in college, and often not even then. It's too bad. Their parents should have helped them find Jesus and His motivating power of love and grace as soon as the children could begin to grasp it.

So let's not use Ellen G. White to teach our children correct behavior without the love and the power of Jesus Christ. Morality by itself for righteousness is useless to God. In fact, I would like to take the position that God never uses righteousness by works to lead to righteousness by faith because it is antagonistic to the very principles of His plan. Would God use a principle or method opposed to His ultimate goal to get us there? We're the ones who've fallen into the trap of thinking that way. He shows us the uselessness of our works only so that we will recognize our need of Him. Christ meets us where we are, and when we see how futile our external goodness is, then we will seek

Him (see Matthew 19:16-20).

The idea that God expects us to force ourselves to obey until we reach the ultimate experience of Christian maturity in which we'll do so naturally rests upon another false premise: that impulsive obedience is a "goal" that we'll eventually attain when we're 30, 40, 50, or maybe 80. If we diagramed the concept, it might look something like this:

We will call it a "sin seismograph." Let's assume that before we become Christians, whenever we lose our temper the needle on the meter jumps to 10 on the scale. As we begin and continue the Christian life the idea is that gradually the needle drops lower and lower on the scale. Perhaps after a year or two the needle will only rise to 8 when we get angry. Then after several more years of "trying hard" it may go up to only 6 in times of stress. The idea is that through a lifetime of "diligent effort" we may hope to get in before we die at least one good day when the needle won't even move under stress and temptation.

But God has provided a better way—that our growth is in the *constancy* of our total surrender or dependence on Him. The final victories of ultimate faith the Christian can experience during part of every day, *right now*, whether or not he has just about lived his Christian lifetime. In other words, you can know the complete victories that come through total dependence upon God some portion (hopefully more and more) of every day, so that the natural obedience available to the mature Christian *all* the time *is* available now, but experienced by the infant Christian *part* of the time. The "sin seismograph" would then look like this:

Notice that it now has only two positions on its scale: 0 and 10. Whether I've been a Christian for one week or for eighty years, whenever I depend on myself under stress and temptation, the needle gets pinned at 10 every time. On the other hand, whenever I am in total reliance on God's power, the needle doesn't even flicker.

Now let's put it together. The genuine Christian's ongoing relationship with God we will represent with a circle:

Within it we find the painful swing back and forth between dependence on God's power and upon self:

At any moment of stress and temptation that we rest in His power, the needle on the meter doesn't even tremble:

But at any moment of stress and temptation that we retreat back to our own strength, the needle shoots over to 10:

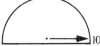

The increasing *constancy* of zero would indicate growth in the Christian life.

Wouldn't it be wonderful to surrender and submit in

such constancy now that we would lock in on it twenty-four hours tomorrow and for the rest of our lives? It *is* God's will. Let's not think that God *wants* us to take a lifetime before we can experience total surrender all the time. We don't believe that if we haven't been Christians *long* enough God will allow us to experience total victory over known sin only one hour a day. God's plan is to give us *total, absolute victory twenty-four hours right now.*

But what's the problem? It's our stubborn resistance— wanting to do it ourselves and to live in some sense apart from Him instead of completely submitting to His control. That's why we go through the painful growth of learning to depend totally upon God more and more constantly each day. It teaches us that constant dependence is *God's* work, because no one "can empty himself of self. . . . [He] can only consent for Christ to accomplish the work" (*Christ's Object Lessons*, p. 159). Our part is to consent by opening the door day by day for continuing fellowship and communion through our choice of the private devotional life with God.

Ellen G. White writes in *Steps to Christ*, page 61, that "if we abide in Christ, if the love of God dwells in us, our feelings, our thoughts, our purposes, our actions, will be in harmony with the will of God." This is obviously something more than simply external morality or obedience, for it includes our feelings, thoughts, motives, as well. Elsewhere she states, "Through faith, every deficiency of character may be supplied, every defilement cleansed, every fault corrected, every excellence developed" (*The Acts of the Apostles*, p. 564).

Christ will purify our tastes, inclinations, affections, motives (*Gospel Workers*, p. 127); our thoughts and desires (*Prophets and Kings*, p. 233); our inherent selfishness (*The Desire of Ages*, p. 678); our minds and hearts (*ibid.*, p. 176); our aims and impulses (*ibid.*, p. 668). He will change our tendencies (*SDA Bible Commentary*, Vol. 6, p. 1101); subdue our ambitions and passions (*Review and Herald*, July 2, 1889); remold our spirits, characters—which include the whole man—our dispositions, feelings, and emotions (*SDA Bible Commentary*, Vol. 6, p. 1080); and finally, He will transform our imaginations (*The Acts of the Apostles*, pp. 482, 483).

Then if the renewing, transforming power of the indwelling Christ, who wants to take control, changes our inner selves, would we still have to try hard to do what's right? Isn't it safe to conclude that we'd have to try hard *not* to? Let's not cheapen God's grace and His plan by saying that He helps us grit our teeth and struggle more diligently to be good through our own deliberate efforts.

Does it mean that God offers strength and gives us the option to use what we need? No. God offers *Himself* to come and live His life in and through us so that *He* wills and does in us. "When the heart is open to Jesus, and the mind responds to the truth, Jesus abides in the soul. The Spirit's energy works in the heart, and leads the inclinations toward Jesus. By living faith, the Christian places entire dependence on divine power, expecting that *God will will and do* that which is according to His good pleasure" (*Signs of the Times*, June 4, 1912, italics supplied).

If I'll choose the experience of letting *God* work in me, then He will control me in my other choices. He'll also back up those choices with all the power of heaven. Thus victory is possible. "Man, fallen man, may be transformed by the renewing of the mind. . . . How . . . ? By the Holy Spirit taking possession of his mind, spirit, heart, and character. . . . Just as a good tree will bear good fruit, so will the tree that is actually planted in the Lord's garden produce good fruit unto eternal life" (*SDA Bible Commentary*, Vol. 6, p. 1080).

Notice what happens as a result: "Besetting sins are

overcome; evil thoughts are not allowed in the mind; evil habits are purged from the soul temple. The tendencies which have been biased in a wrong direction are turned in a right direction. Wrong dispositions and feelings are changed, new principles of action supplied, and there is a new standard of character. Holy tempers and sanctified emotions are now the fruit borne upon the Christian tree. An entire transformation has taken place. This is the work to be wrought" *(ibid.)*.

So there is work to accomplish, but does it sound like our doing? Are we supposed to use our human effort toward this? "We see by experience that in our own human strength, resolutions and purposes are of no avail. Must we, then, give up our determined efforts? No; although our experience testifies that we cannot possibly do this work ourselves, help has been laid upon One who is mighty *to do it for us*. But the only way we can secure the help of God is to put ourselves wholly in His hands, and trust Him to work for us. As we lay hold of Him by faith, *He does the work*. The believer can only trust" *(ibid.,* italics supplied).

"Man is given the privilege of working with God in the saving of his own soul. He is to receive Christ as his personal Saviour and believe in Him. Receiving and believing is his part of the contract" *(Review and Herald,* May 28, 1908).

That's all that man can do—He can trust and depend on God. After he has received Christ as his personal Saviour and *continues* to accept Him, believing through personal communication each day that God is able, he has done his part of the contract. That's what some people would call the ultimate heresy in salvation by faith, but I believe it is the truth. Only one thing can we do to be saved *from* our sins and to keep saved in the ongoing Christian life. It is the only thing that so many of us have not done—and that is spending time alone with Christ at the beginning of every day for continual fellowship, communication, and communion throughout the day. That's all we can do. And if we use our will and willpower toward knowing Christ as our personal Saviour, Lord, and Friend, He will do the rest for us, in and through us. The reason we have met with defeat in our "duty and deliberate obedience" approach is because we don't believe God will do it for us. Sure, it is an effectual blow to our pride, but God's plan of salvation has no room for man's pride.

Is the human will important in the life of the Christian? "Let no man present the idea that man has little or nothing to do in the great work of overcoming; for God does nothing for man without his cooperation. Neither say that after you have done all you can on your part, Jesus will help you. Christ has said, 'Without me ye can do nothing' (John 15:5)" (*Selected Messages*, Book One, p. 381).

So what is the role of our will in salvation? Sometimes we think there are many things *we* have to do in living the Christian life, and we wear out our lives trying to accomplish them. But I will never forget the thrill and the relief that came to me when I realized that what God really expected me to do, consciously and deliberately, was to make use of the avenues He has provided by which I may keep in touch with Him, His righteousness, and His power: Bible study and prayer. Through those simple, yet often neglected, means He comes into close fellowship with us and fulfills the mystery of the gospel, "Christ *in* you" (Colossians 1:27; see also 2 Corinthians 5:17). The devotional life is not something we do in addition to being a Christian. It is not optional, for it is the entire basis of the continuing Christian life.

What is the nature of our devotional life? Do we take it for granted too much? Do we know what it means to trust in

God? And do we know what it means to spend a thoughtful hour in personal fellowship with Jesus Christ each morning, contemplating His life and teachings as they apply to *us* for that day? If not, we'll never know victory.

Chapter 5

Where the Battle Isn't

Near the town of Huelva on the southern coast of Spain lies a British subject named William Martin. He never knew the great contribution he made to the outcome of World War II, especially in Sicily, because he died of pneumonia in the foggy dampness of England before he ever saw the battlefront.

The Allies had had a plan for him, necessitated by the acuteness of the hour. They put him in ice while it developed.

The Allied forces had invaded North Africa, and their next logical step was to move into Sicily, an idea already anticipated by the Germans. To reach bases in North Africa the British flew their officers and orders around the southern coast of neutral Spain. Knowing that the Germans were aware of it as well, the Allies decided to outfox them. So they proceeded with their plans for Major William Martin.

One dark night a submarine came to the surface just off the coast of Spain and let the body of William Martin out into the sea. Also it turned loose a rubber raft and one oar. The dead man's pocket contained secret documents which indicated that the next Allied move would be to strike in Greece and Sardinia. It was a shot in the dark, but the body of William Martin washed ashore as did the raft.

The Axis intelligence in neutral territory soon found the papers and assumed that William Martin had perished in a crash at sea. The documents passed through the Axis officers' hands all the way to Hitler's headquarters. As a result, the Germans transferred thousands of men from Sicily to Greece and Sardinia—where the battle wasn't— and the Allied forces moved into Sicily.

Here we have an illustration of the dilemma of thousands of Christians. How many of us are fighting where the battle isn't instead of where it is?

In previous chapters we have discussed the necessity of letting God will and do in us. But the idea leads some to rightly protest, "There has to be something in the Christian life that involves action, willpower, effort, and discipline. Don't say that we have nothing to do in the Christian life except to let Jesus do it *all* while we sit and rock." I'd like to concur that the Christian life demands every ounce of backbone and effort and discipline a person can muster—*where the battle is.*

I wish that we could clearly understand where the battle takes place. The Bible tells us to "fight the good fight of faith, lay hold on eternal life, whereunto thou art also called, and hast professed a good profession before many witnesses" (1 Timothy 6:12). Are we supposed to combat the enemy? Or do we engage in the fight of faith? Is there a difference between the fight of faith and the fight of sin?

Let's imagine that we have two groups of people— Group A and Group B. All of the people in Group A participate in the fight of faith. They try to know God personally, spending time in prayer each day and searching to understand God's Word for the purpose of communication with Him. Group A seeks a definite, meaningful, growing relationship with Christ day by day. That is the fight of faith.

In contrast, all of the members of Group B wage the fight of sin. Trying to live a good life through their own efforts, they work hard to overcome their evil habits and practice. Their attention is on the enemy, and they're struggling diligently. Some of them fail and become discouraged. Others "succeed," and they're proud. Their fight centers where the battle *isn't*.

"Oh," says someone, "wait a minute. Doesn't the Bible say, 'Resist the devil, and he will flee from you'?" Yes, it does in James 4:7. But *how* are we supposed to do it? By battling against sin and the devil? No. By submitting to God, by waging the fight of faith.

The fight of faith takes every ounce of energy, self-discipline, and willpower, every bit of human effort that we can muster. God does expect us to engage in this battle, but He does not expect *us* to fight *sin*.

Ephesians 6:10-18 describes the Christian warfare: "Finally, my brethren, be strong in the Lord, and in the power of his might. Put on the whole armour of God, that ye may be able to stand against the wiles of the devil. For we wrestle not against flesh and blood, but against principalities, against powers, against the rulers of the darkness of this world, against spiritual wickedness in high places. Wherefore take unto you the whole armour of God, that ye may be able to withstand in the evil day, and having done all, *to stand*.

"Stand therefore, having your loins girt about with truth, and having on the breastplate of righteousness; and your feet shod with the preparation of the gospel of peace; above all, taking the shield of faith, wherewith ye shall be able to quench all the fiery darts of the wicked. And take the helmet of salvation, and the sword of the Spirit, which is the word of God: praying always with all prayer and supplication in the Spirit, and watching thereunto with all perseverance and supplication for all saints."

Notice the phrases that Paul uses to portray the battle. Is he talking about Group A or Group B? "Finally, my brethren, be strong. . . ." Group B leaps up and says, "Amen. That's it. That's ammunition for our side. We have to be strong and fight the enemy." But wait a minute. The entire phrase says, *"Be strong in the Lord."* And Group A immediately proclaims, "That's for our side. We're supposed to be strong *in Him* and in the power of *His* might."

Let's continue reading a little farther: "Put on the whole armour of God." Group B declares, "There it is again. *We* have to put on the armor so that *we* can fight." But Paul then describes the armor of God as being *truth, faith, the Holy Spirit,* and *righteousness.* Only one kind of righteousness exists, and that we find in Christ. What is the armor of God? It is the *spiritual* armor that Group A seeks. "Put on the whole armour of God, . . . for we wrestle not against flesh and blood, but against . . . [wicked spirits] in high places."

I remember meeting a former boxer who had become a follower of Christ. He told me, "If we could only get the devil out in the open, I'd be happy to land one on his jaw. If only I could flatten him to the ground. But that's what's frustrating about the Christian life. We can't get him out in the open."

Now if the battle that I'm engaged in has to do with spirits, what is my only hope for victory? Can flesh and blood fight spirits? Have you ever tried it? It's like shadowboxing. There's no way you can win. If the conflict involves spirits, then the only possible thing for me to do is to engage another Spirit to fight for me. "Bear in mind that it is none but God that can hold an argument with Satan" (*SDA Bible Commentary,* Vol. 5, p. 1083).

The Bible says that "God is a Spirit" (John 4:24), that the

angels are "ministering spirits" (Hebrews 1:13, 14), and we speak much about the Holy Spirit. Then what is my challenge? It is for me to participate in the fight of faith, the effort to know God personally, to turn the war over to Him. God invites me to enlist in the fight of faith, not the fight of sin. And yet, it seems, among young and old alike, we find a great tendency to think of the Christian life in terms of the latter.

The fight of sin is not where the battle really is regardless of whether I've been seemingly "successful" or not, because the only way I can ever succeed in it is externally, outwardly, and that means nothing in God's book. Of course it impresses the courts of the land, it works with the traffic signals and police on the highways, and it keeps me out of jail, but it does not count for Christianity or for salvation.

You see, the people in Group B are good moralists. They would never do anything to hurt anybody else intentionally. But they're good and moral in their own strength, through their own self-discipline. *Outwardly* they're Christians. But they're not relying on God for power and strength. In contrast, the people in Group A know that self-discipline toward overcoming things externally is not where the battle is. The difference between the fight of sin and the fight of faith constitutes one of the greatest truths for the discouraged Christian to learn. The person who has discovered it and has experienced the fight of faith and the rewards that come from knowing God is the one who begins to shout it from the housetops.

Ellen White has commented that the fight of sin is the wrong thing to focus on because "no mere external change is sufficient to bring us into harmony with God. There are many who try to reform by correcting this or that bad habit, and they hope in this way to become Christians, but they are beginning in the wrong place. Our first work is with the heart" (*Christ's Object Lessons*, p. 97).

I'd also like to remind you of another passage that I quoted in a previous chapter, but which I would like to repeat here: "There are those who profess to serve God, while they rely upon their own efforts to obey His law, to form a right character, and secure salvation. Their hearts are not moved by any deep sense of the love of Christ, but they seek to perform the duties of the Christian life as that which God requires of them in order to gain heaven. *Such religion is worth nothing*" (*Steps to Christ*, p. 44, italics supplied).

Can't I have even a little bit of credit? No. Then where should I be placing my will and my willpower? Toward working on the rules, regulations, and laws for salvation? Toward the fight of sin? No. My battle is in the area of constant relationship and dependence, in a one-to-one involvement with God.

Ellen White also states that "sinful man can find hope and righteousness only in God, and no human being is righteous any longer than he has faith in God and maintains a vital connection with Him" (*Testimonies to Ministers*, p. 367). Then the weapons that Paul describes in Ephesians are the right ones, because they deal with the battle where the battle is.

Now notice three different approaches to the Christian life. First, we encounter the person who accepts God's plan, he thinks, but he launches into the fight of sin as the basis of his Christian experience. Second, we meet someone who begins to realize that the *relationship* with Christ is an important factor. He seeks God while still trying to fight the enemy. His is a half-and-half experience, a transitional stage that most of us go through. The third approach is God's ultimate plan—a concept that we should understand in theory, even if we haven't experienced it yet—to wage the fight of *faith* with *all* of our willpower. As we learn to concentrate our efforts toward growing in spiritual relationship, *God* takes over the battle with the enemy. *God* fights for us.

But that second example is a common problem. God has promised to fight our battles for us, but we don't always seem to believe it. The greatest battle ever fought is to realize in our own minds that God is able to fulfill His promises.

In his book *Captains of the Host*, Arthur Spalding discusses some of the problems of the Christian experience. Climaxing them all, he says, "Far more subtle is the conviction set in the minds of most professed Christians . . . that man must strive to be good and to do good, and that when he has done all he can, Christ will come to his aid and help him to do the rest. In this confused credo of salvation partly by works and partly with auxiliary power, many trust today" (p. 601).

Ellen White describes the same problem: "[Some] think they are committing themselves to God, [while] there is a great deal of self-dependence. There are conscientious souls that trust partly to God, and partly to themselves. . . . There are no victories in this kind of faith. Such persons toil to no purpose; their souls are in continual bondage, and they find no rest until their burdens are laid at the feet of Jesus" (*Selected Messages*, Book One, p. 353).

"Each one will have a close struggle to overcome sin in his own heart. This is at times a very painful and discouraging work; because, as we see the deformities in our character, we keep looking at them, when we should look to Jesus and put on the robe of His righteousness. Everyone who enters the pearly gates of the city of God will enter there as a conqueror, and his greatest conquest will have been the conquest of self [not things]" (*Testimonies for the Church*, Vol. 9, pp. 182, 183). In another place she states that "we are not to look at ourselves. The more we dwell upon our own imperfections, the less strength we shall have to overcome them" (*Review and Herald*, January 14, 1890).

Dividing my time between the fight of sin and the fight of faith is not God's plan for me. It must be *all* of my effort directed toward the fight of faith. That's where the battle really is, and it will take every ounce of energy and self-discipline that I can produce. If I'm weak, God will meet me more than halfway. Then He fights *for* me my battle with the enemy.

For example, I might choose to fly to Hawaii. So I make my way down to a California beach. There, running as fast as I can, I begin flopping my arms in the breeze, hoping to embark on my trip to Waikiki. Yet I can flap them all day long and far into the night, but I will never leave the ground. In fact, I may be so tired when I have finished trying to fly by myself that I may not have enough strength left to get over to the airport.

However, if I will choose *not* to do something I cannot do, but will rather choose to do something I *can* do—putting myself in the hands of a pilot on a plane bound for Hawaii—it is safe to conclude that I will arrive at my destination. Once I have made that choice, the pilot will do the rest for me. "Man is not able to save himself, but the Son of God *fights his battles for him*, and places him on vantage-ground by *giving* him his divine attributes" (*Review and Herald*, February 8, 1898, italics supplied).

Translated into real life, what is God trying to tell us? He's saying that if we will choose to fight the fight of faith, with *all* of our willpower properly directed to the real source of power in our lives, we will conquer (see

Testimonies for the Church, Vol. 5, p. 513). If we will concentrate whatever willpower we have in the direction of knowing Jesus personally and allowing Him to live His life within, then we will succeed. Our self-discipline we use in choosing a daily personal relationship with God. Then we must leave our battles against our sins, our problems, to Him. Here is one of the hardest ideas for human beings to accept, probably because of humanity's natural pride and self-sufficiency. We cherish the thought that we can do more if we try harder.

Many people have gotten the impression that Ellen G. White was primarily concerned with the fight of sin. But the only reason for her many volumes is to tell us that the enemy approaches and to drive us to our knees for the fight of faith. Don't ever forget that. "God rebukes His people for their sins, that He may humble them, and lead them to seek His face" (*Review and Herald,* February 25, 1902).

With Paul's description of the Christian warfare in Ephesians, let's couple an Old Testament battle—a humorous, intriguing one that appears in 2 Chronicles, chapter 20. The Moabites and the Ammonites came up to Judah to do battle with God's people. The king of Judah at that time was Jehoshaphat, a good king. (In fact, he was so busy being a good ruler that his son Jehoram became bad.)

King Jehoshaphat received the news: "The enemy is coming!" What did he do? Call out the militia? declare a state of emergency? sharpen spears? get out on the target range with the bows and arrows? prepare for armed confrontation with the enemy?

No. Jehoshaphat knew that wasn't where the battle was. Instead, he realized how to fight where the conflict really was. Notice what he did. He "set himself to seek the Lord, and proclaimed a fast throughout all Judah," and the people gathered themselves together "out of all the cities of

Judah . . . to seek the Lord" (verses 3, 4). They had a prayer meeting. Doesn't that seem like an irrational way to defend themselves? But that's what they did.

It's interesting to read their prayer. So often our prayers insult God. We rush into His presence with demands: "God, I need this. I need that. I've got a problem with this and a problem with that. Do this for me. Give me this and give me that." But those people didn't pray that way. They knelt down and said, "Lord, You're the one who's in charge. You're the great God, the God of Abraham, Isaac, and Jacob. You're the one with all the power." They spent time giving praise, honor, and glory to God. And at the end of their prayer they said, "Now, we've got a problem, Lord. The enemy is coming. We don't have any might against their forces. But we're looking to *You* for help." What type of conflict was that? the fight of sin? No. It was the fight of faith. *"Our eyes are upon thee"* (verse 12).

Didn't they have *any* might? Couldn't they have finished off *some* of the enemy? Certainly. They could have done *something*. But Jehoshaphat knew that wasn't God's plan. The Lord never expected them to engage with the enemy. He promised to wage their battles for them: "Ye shall not fear them: for the Lord your God he shall fight for you" (Deuteronomy 3:22).

And as they prayed, saying, "Our eyes are upon thee," a man suddenly jumped up in the middle of the congregation. But he wasn't like the demoniac who interrupted the church services at Capernaum. Jahaziel wasn't a fanatic or a loudmouth. He was a man on whom, obviously, the Spirit of God rested, for he began to prophesy: "Harken ye, all Judah, and ye inhabitants of Jerusalem, and thou king Jehoshaphat, Thus saith the Lord unto you, Be not afraid nor dismayed by reason of this great multitude; for *the battle is not your's, but God's*. To morrow go ye down against them. . . . *Ye shall not need to fight in this battle:* set yourselves, stand ye still, and see the salvation of the Lord with you, O Judah and Jerusalem: fear not, nor be dismayed; to morrow go out against them: for the Lord will be with you" (2 Chronicles 20:15-17).

Again, as with Paul's description in Ephesians, it would be possible for both those in the fight of sin (Group B) and those in the fight of faith (Group A) to say that the message applied to their side.

"Be not afraid nor dismayed; . . . for the battle is not your's, but God's." Sounds like support for Group A, doesn't it?

"To morrow go ye down against them." "Right!" says Group B. "That's it, now. You've got to add your human effort alongside the power of God."

But what were they to go out and do? "Ye shall not need to fight in this battle: set yourselves, stand ye still." Ephesians 6:11 states, "Put on the whole armour of God, that ye may be able to *stand.*"

"Stand ye still, and see the salvation of the Lord." Jehoshaphat hadn't quite been used to fighting his battles that way before, so he tried to think of a way to accomplish the feat of standing still to watch the salvation of the Lord. Finally he had a bright idea. He'd send out the choir to meet the enemy.

Now, of course, that didn't seem too sensible. In the first place, I'm not sure the choir members completely favored his plan. And in the second place, sending out a choir to meet the enemy would make them much angrier. It would seem that it would so insult the enemy that they'd try to wipe the entire people of God off the face of the earth, starting with the choir. But that was the plan, and the choir apparently agreed to carry it through.

I can just see them the next day—all of them—going out

with the choir members wearing their robes, leading the procession, and singing. And they weren't even singing battle hymns. They sang a doxology: "Praise the Lord; for his mercy endureth for ever" (verse 21).

As they went out there with the others following, what happened? Can't you just picture the enemy's reaction as they come around the mountain there in the wilderness only to hear the strains of praise? It infuriates them, and they shout, "Let's hurry up and get there as fast as we can! We'll finish these people off in short order."

Meanwhile, in the choir I can see a man who has brought along his bow and arrows underneath his robe—a man in the back row. Now, I want you to notice that the strange battle involved not attacking the enemy and, in fact, not even *fighting* him. I'd like to suggest that many people, young and old alike, have discovered the tragic trap that the enemy has prepared for us—that he defeats us by directing our attention to him and to our reactions to him. That's where the defeat lies. But here, in the Old Testament, is a sample of God's way for victory—through keeping our eyes on Him.

Watch the man in the back row. He sees the enemy rounding the corner, getting closer and closer, and he starts reasoning in his own mind, "I can draw a bead over the shoulder of the first bass in front of me and finish off one of the Moabites. And then I think I can shoot another one before they all get here." It's the same temptation that you and I face today—to fight the battle where it isn't, to do something ourselves.

But, instead, what happened? Evidently he kept his bow and arrows beneath his choir robe, and when they began to sing praises to God, the Lord sent ambushes against Ammon and Moab. The Edomites suddenly came in with a surprise flank movement. The Ammonites,

Moabites, and Edomites found themselves involved in a battle before they ever reached God's people. They continued fighting until they got confused. Pretty soon the Ammonites and the Moabites engaged each other instead of the Edomites, and the confusion and conflict continued until finally, when Judah came upon the scene and looked at the battlefield, "behold, they were dead bodies fallen to the earth, and none escaped" (verse 24).

What are we supposed to learn from the story? That we must depend upon Christ alone for our salvation from the enemy.

I wish it were possible for me to transfer immediately from Group B (depending on self to fight the enemy) to Group A (depending on God within the fight of *faith*) without going through a half-and-half experience in my life. I've discovered that it is usual for me to swing back and forth from Group A to Group B even during the course of a given day. And I need more than anything else to grow in my relationship with Christ to the point where I let Him do it all instead of my getting mixed up in the battle and trying to do part of it myself.

An old church hymnal had a song that died a long time ago. One day I sat down at the piano and discovered why—it had a horrible tune. But the words are tremendous. It describes the process of switching from Group B to Group A. When a person first begins to turn toward God before conversion, he depends upon himself: "All of self and none of Thee." Then he finds Christ and says, "Some of self and some of Thee." But as he continues to grow in his Christian experience, in his personal relationship with God, he sings, "Less of self and more of Thee." And finally he concludes, "None of self and all of Thee." That is what I need in my own life. One of my greatest temptations as a minister is to look at the tremendous challenge around me and to start trying to do something myself.

The only reason to recognize the tremendous challenge in the church and community is *not* so that we can try to figure out some clever maneuver or exciting entertainment to draw crowds. It is to send us to our knees to pray for spiritual breakthrough in our community and everywhere else. May God deliver us from resorting to man-made gimmicks to do His work.

So wherever the battle is, whether it's a struggle against the enemy and sin or whether it's in terms of trying to finish God's work in our world, the real challenge is *not* to create more gimmicks, techniques, or humanistic methods. The challenge to us today is to send us to our knees where "our eyes are upon . . . [God]."

Chapter 6

Jesus—Controlled by God

Thus far in our study of the will we have concentrated on an understanding of the *theory* of God's plan for our effort, our power of choice, our willpower. "But," some may object, "that sounds too idealistic. No one can live that way in everyday *experience*." But Jesus—our greatest single example of how to use our will and our willpower in the Christian life—has shown us that it is possible.

John 14 relates how Jesus sat with His disciples in the upper room, teaching them before His crucifixion. And then Philip asked Jesus to show them the Father. Perhaps his question was idle curiosity, perhaps it was more than that. Jesus replied, "Have I been so long time with you, and yet hast thou not known me, Philip? . . . [We're the same. If you've seen Me, you've seen the Father]" (verse 9). He continued, "Believest thou not that I am in the Father, and the Father in me? the words that I speak unto you I speak not of myself: but the Father that dwelleth in me, he doeth the works" (verse 10).

Some people have argued that Jesus had an advantage because of His divinity, that He used His divine nature to live His perfect life on earth. But I would like to suggest that Jesus might have been at a disadvantage because He did *not* use His inherent divinity. And if Jesus lived His victorious life by relying solely on His Father, then, through Him, all the power of Heaven is at our disposal too, and we can have victories the way that Jesus had.

Who did the works in Jesus' life according to His statement in John 14:10? Sure, it was Jesus' hands, feet, eyes, and mouth, but somehow it was His Father doing all of it through Him, in Him. Not even His words were His own (John 12:49). It probably isn't any easier to grasp how this happened than it is to explain that God wants to dwell in us so that *He* wills and does in us. But nonetheless, that's the way it is. Christ's statement should eliminate any debate left on the meaning of Philippians 2:13—that *God* does the willing and the doing in us. If you would transpose the text to Jesus' life, you would hear Him saying, "My Father is willing and doing within Me; He's the One who is doing the works."

Jesus' life is the greatest example of total, absolute surrender, of submission by His own choice, as He placed Himself under the control of His Father. And we've already noticed in an earlier chapter that such guidance is not dangerous to our freedom because it is the control of *love*. Christ subjected Himself to the control of His Father's love. Therefore His Father spoke the words and did the works in Jesus' life.

The human will should operate the same way in the postconversion Christian experience. Instead of occupying itself with doing or not doing this or that work, or with saying this or that thing, it should seek the relationship of absolute dependence upon God. Jesus explained God's plan for each of us: "Believe me that I am in the Father, and the Father in me: or else believe me for the very works' sake. Verily, verily, I say unto you, He that believeth on me, the works that I do shall he do also; and greater works than these shall he do; because I go unto my Father. And whatsoever ye shall ask in my name, that will I do, that the

Father may be glorified in the Son" (John 14:11-13).

Notice His promise: "Whatever you ask in my name, I will do it" (verse 13, RSV). Some have interpreted it to mean that if you mouth the name of Jesus, you can obtain anything you want—get your tuition paid, find your glasses, receive a new Lincoln Continental. The name of Jesus thus becomes a magical formula. But what does it involve to pray in the name of Jesus? *The Desire of Ages* tells us that it means "to accept *His* character, manifest *His* spirit, and work *His* works" (p. 668, italics supplied).

"To pray in the name of Jesus is something more than a mere mention of that name at the beginning and the ending of a prayer. It is to pray in the mind and spirit of Jesus, while we believe *His* promises, rely upon *His* grace, and work *His* works" (*Steps to Christ*, pp. 100, 101, italics supplied).

If you'll study the context of Jesus' statement, you'll discover that it means to allow Jesus to pray through you, in you, from the position of subjection and His absolute control. If Jesus guides my life, then who motivates my praying? And if He is in control, you can be certain that I am going to pray the right prayer and ask because of the right reasons. The only person who can pray in the name of Jesus is the one who prays from the standpoint of utter dependence and relationship with Jesus, just as Jesus prayed to His Father.

Then if this is true, how did Jesus live His life in our world? If His life is to be our example, He must have lived in a way possible for us.

I used to think mistakenly that Jesus had the advantage over me in living a perfect life because He was born inherently divine as well as human, and the rest of us can't make that claim. But I'd like to illustrate the way He lived His perfect life by a diagram:

Letting the circle represent Jesus, we then divide it into half and label one side "human" and the other "divine." Of course we don't believe that the left half of Jesus was human and the right divine. I am getting literal only for the sake of illustration. The truth is that Jesus was all human and all divine. If the circle represented us, we would put in no dividing line at all. We would be all human, and if you haven't discovered that yet, then you're not human.

Of course, Jesus was born different. He had a sinless human nature, the same as Adam had before his fall, *concerning propensity or tendency to sin.* Therefore it was natural for Jesus to be good. I was born with a sinful nature, and it's natural for me to be bad.

But Jesus did not rely upon, nor did He use, the divine part of His nature to live His perfect life. Remember He said, "I can of mine own self do nothing" (John 5:[19,] 30). If He had been talking about possibilities or potential, then it would not have been an accurate statement.

As God, He could have done plenty—things that you or I could never conceive of doing, and He could have accomplished them by Himself, apart from dependence on His Father. Have you ever had to resist the temptation to turn stones into bread? I've struggled with a lot of things but never that one. Could you ever say, "I have power to lay . . . [my life] down, and I have power to take it again"? Jesus could (John 10:18), and, in fact, He raised Himself on the resurrection morning. The angel merely brought permission from His Father (*The Desire of Ages,* p. 785).

Let's take a closer look at the temptation of Christ in the wilderness as recorded in Luke 4. Jesus fasted there for almost six weeks, and Satan appeared to tempt Him to turn stones into bread. The devil knows there is no point in trying to induce me to transform stones into bread, because he recognizes that I'm not capable of it anyway. But he knew that Jesus was born with the kind of power in which He could have done it, even without depending on His Father. What was the issue? To do something wrong? No. It was to do something right. Satan tempted Jesus to change the stones into homemade, stone-ground bread. Is it wrong to eat old-fashioned homemade bread after you've fasted for forty days? I've polished off half a loaf after skipping a few meals. And I didn't feel too sinful about it either. It's not a sin to be hungry when you haven't eaten for nearly six weeks.

So what was the real issue in the temptation? We often say appetite, and of course it was involved here, but that was not the primary one at all. The fundamental issue centered on Jesus' doing something on His own, *good or bad*, using His inherent divinity instead of relying upon God. Satan tempted Him to prove His own divinity, to do it by Himself, independent of His Father. And Jesus *could* have used His own power, but He came to earth to show us how to surrender our own strength and rely upon God's instead. In His total reliance on His Father, Jesus said in effect, "I am here to demonstrate to man how to live through dependence upon a higher power. My Father has not seen fit to provide Me with bread yet, and if it is His will that I starve to death, that's all right with Me. In the meantime, until He sends Me bread, I'll go hungry. I will not rely on My own powers."

The experience offers the classic example of how to live the Christian life. It was natural for Jesus to do good (outwardly and inwardly). He had no propensities to evil. Evil was repulsive to Him. And therefore the "bad" that

Satan tempted Him to do was to utilize His own powers (which would not have failed Him) to do something good. The fantastic truth is that He did not rely upon Himself, and therefore all His deeds came from God. As Christ lived in dependence upon God, so we can live in dependence on Christ (John 17:23).

Going back, then, to the diagram we used earlier, just put a big black X through the divine part of Jesus' life, for He did not use it. Through His human nature, in the same way that you and I must live, He relied upon divine power from *above* instead of divine power from *within*. Thus His life would look like this: **GOD**

The divinity demonstrated in the life of Jesus came from His Father. It was not His own. And the power that He had is available to you and me today.

Jesus in His death could not save Himself. And yet, what would have happened if we had been in His place at His trial when they, spitting, slapping, and jeering, imbedded the crown of thorns deeper into His brow? How easy it would have been to say, "It's about time we showed these people just who it is they're pushing around!" But Jesus did not come to save Himself, and in Gethsemane, His trial, and His death—at no time did He ever tap His divine nature to save Himself or to relieve His physical suffering and anguish. When the priests shook their heads at the cross, saying, "He saved others; himself He [could] . . . not save," it was true. It was the gospel in one sentence.

The same truth applies to His life, too, for it was an integral part of the plan of salvation that Jesus live in the same way that we must, with no supernatural advantage. Therefore He could not save Himself. But look at the methods we've devised to try to save ourselves. Instead, we could be following Jesus' example of dependence on His Father. No wonder Jesus is the greatest single example of salvation by faith. Thus "unless He [Jesus] met man as man, and testified by His connection with God that divine power was not given to Him in a different way to what it will be given to us, He could not be a perfect example for us" (*SDA Bible Commentary*, Vol. 7, p. 925).

"He endured every trial to which we are subject. And He exercised in His own behalf no power that is not freely offered to us. As man, He met temptation, and overcame in the strength given Him from God" (*The Desire of Ages*, p. 24).

"Wait!" someone protests. "What about those miracles He performed? Virtue went out of Him when the woman touched the hem of His garment. He made people whole [Matthew 9:20-22; Mark 6:56]. Wasn't that something special and divine?" Haven't you ever heard of Paul and the handkerchiefs? You can read about it in Acts 19:12, the *SDA Bible Commentary*, Vol. 6, p. 1064, and *Sketches From the Life of Paul*, p. 135.

"Well, but He raised the dead" (Luke 7:1-15; John 11:44), another observes. So did His followers (Acts 9:36-42).

"He read people's minds" (Luke 7:39-47; John 4:29). So did His disciples (Acts 5:3).

"What about the time in Nazareth when He disappeared?" (Luke 4:29, 30). Remember the story of Philip in the desert (Acts 8:39)?

If you study everything usually considered a demonstration of Christ's divinity, you will discover that His followers did the same things—opening the eyes of the blind, casting out devils, healing the sick, walking on the water.

The greatest proof of His inherent divinity was not what He did; it's what He said and what His Father said about Him. On occasion Jesus spoke as God, telling them that He was the Messiah (John 4:26), and a few times His Father testified to His Sonship from heaven (Matthew 3:17; John 12:28). But He *lived* as a man. And the things His Father did in Him are possible for Jesus to do in us through the relationship of dependence.

"Christ in His life on earth made no plans for Himself. He accepted God's plans for Him, and day by day the Father unfolded His plans. So should we depend upon God, that our lives may be the simple outworking of His will. As we commit our ways to Him, He will direct our steps" (*The Ministry of Healing,* p. 479).

Always "the Son of God was surrendered to the Father's will, and dependent upon His power. So utterly was Christ emptied of self that He made no plans for Himself. He accepted God's plans for Him and day by day the Father unfolded His plans" (*The Desire of Ages,* p. 208).

Immediately you can see that Jesus becomes a mighty argument in favor of the relationship of submission to God's control. When He was out on the lake where the billows cast the boat about, He slept, but not because He was the Master of the earth, sea, and sky (and He *could* have used His own power again) but because He trusted in His Father's might. Since He had laid *down* His almighty power, He could do nothing Himself (John 5:19, 30). *The Desire of Ages* tells us that "it was in faith—faith in God's love and care—that Jesus rested" (p. 336). "The power of the Saviour's Godhead was hidden. He overcame in human nature, relying upon God for power. This is the privilege of all" (*SDA Bible Commentary,* Vol. 5, p. 1108).

Then the power available to Jesus in His way of living also awaits us. Notice the Scripture wording:

Jesus could do nothing by Himself (John 5:30).

We without Christ can do nothing (John 15:5).

Christ was in the Father (John 14:10).

We can be in Christ (2 Corinthians 5:17).

The Father was in Jesus (John 14:10).

Jesus' intent is to be in us (Colossians 1:27).

Jesus did not speak words of Himself (John 14:10).

We do not need to speak for ourselves (Matthew 10:20).

Jesus' Father dwelt in Him (John 14:10).

Christ may dwell in our hearts by faith (Ephesians 3:17).

Even Jesus' miracles were not of His own power. "The miracles of Christ for the afflicted and suffering were wrought by the power of God through the ministration of the angels" (*The Desire of Ages*, p. 143); "it was by faith and prayer that He wrought His miracles" (*ibid.*, p. 536).

Apparently Jesus didn't use His inherent divinity until the morning of the resurrection. Divinity flashed through on occasion as His Father allowed the veil of humanity to slip aside momentarily. But Jesus did not employ it or rely upon it, and divinity from above performed His miracles.

"Well," you might say, "that's all very interesting, but what does it have to do with us? We don't usually have to walk on the water or escape an angry mob by disappearing." True. How does it apply to our trying to live the Christian life? Just this: It is *God's* power, instead of our feeble strength, that meets the temptations of the enemy. *God* fights our battles for us.

If you don't understand that the same power Jesus had from above is also available to us, then expecting to live like Jesus lived could keep you awake at night with worry and frustration. But "Christ . . . withstood the temptation, through the power that man may command. He laid hold on the throne of God, and there is not a man or woman who may not have access to the same help through faith in God. . . .

"Men may have a power to resist evil—a power that neither earth, nor death, nor hell can master; a power that will place them where they may overcome as Christ overcame. Divinity and humanity may be combined in them" (*Review and Herald,* February 18, 1890).

"The Saviour was deeply anxious for His disciples to understand . . . that . . . God was manifested in Him that He might be manifested in them [John 17:23]. Jesus revealed no qualities, and exercised no powers, that men may not have through faith in Him. His perfect humanity is that which all His followers may possess, if they will be in subjection to God as He was" (*The Desire of Ages,* p. 664).

"The life that Christ lived in this world, men and women can live through His power and under His instruction. In their conflict with Satan they may have all the help that He had. They may be more than conquerors through Him who loved them and gave Himself for them" (*Testimonies for the Church,* Vol. 9, p. 22).

"Well," someone else interjects, "Jesus could never have faced temptation the way I do today, because it was natural for Him to be good. And by the time He reached the age of accountability at twelve, He had a perfect record behind Him, while I had already formed sinful habits. How could He suffer and go through conflicts the way I do?" And right here we have to understand the difference between the behaviorist and the relationist when it comes to studying the life and nature of Christ.

The behaviorist—the one who still thinks of sin and temptation in terms of doing bad things—has to have a Lord with the same nature as he has before he can rest or be satisfied. And I've heard people insisting on that. They say,

"Jesus had the *very same* nature that I have, except it was sinless, with no sinful desires or tendencies." That's impossible. It's amazing the extent of mental manipulations that some have performed trying to figure out that paradox. But the behaviorist has to do that—he's the one who gets into the midnight sessions attempting to analyze and dissect Christ's human and divine natures. He's the one who has to have a Saviour who goes through everything he experiences. Otherwise he'll claim that Jesus had an unfair advantage over us and that we can't expect to live victorious lives today.

A careful study will show that Jesus had the nature of man when it came to *physical* infirmities after four thousand years of degeneracy, including mental power and moral worth (*The Desire of Ages*, p. 117). Jesus did not have the physical stamina of Adam. Adam might not have gone to sleep in the bottom of the boat, but Jesus did. In Himself, Jesus was not as smart as Adam, nor did He have as much inherent moral strength as Adam. Then what did Jesus *not* have? He never took on man's sinful propensities. When it came to the desire or the tendency to do evil, Jesus had the absolute, perfect, sinless nature of Adam before he fell. Some theologians debate the subject on and on because they never define their terms. Perhaps the following comparison will help.

How Christ Was Human, As Adam Was:

Before the Fall	After the Fall
No taint of sin in His nature, that is, He had never yielded to sin in actual performance	In a weakened physical organism, thus making the dependence all the more essential

No sinful habits, no "momentum" of sin from past failings	Subject to weariness, hunger
	Separated from the physical presence of the Father
Able to be tempted, able to fall	Surrounded by a corrupt environment that continually brought temptation
Had the innocence of a clear conscience	
	Not as smart as Adam
Never tempted to *continue* in sin	Subject to incessant temptation*
Had through faith maintained an unbroken contact with the Father (submission and dependence)	Willpower was worth far less than Adam's for producing morality or external goodness.

We must never define sin and temptation primarily in terms of behavior. The issue is not of doing right and not doing wrong but of *relationship*. Am I willing to submit to God in dependence, or am I insisting on living independent of God? That's the entire issue. It's what started sin in the first place with Lucifer in heaven, and in the Garden of Eden. If that's true, then Jesus as my example does not have to be a Saviour with sinful propensities to do wrong.

Since the primary issue in temptation is to live in one's strength, who has the bigger temptation to live that way— the one who has never sinned, who has a perfect record

---

*Christ's temptations were *not* like ours in the sense that He found sinning desirable (as we so often do), but most profoundly like ours in a much more basic sense: He was constantly tempted to break the relationship of dependence and submission and to "go it alone" on His own strength. Indeed, it was a more severe temptation for Him, since He actually *had* the power to do so. Yet that is the same point where Satan hits us—breaking the relationship. Fully establishing that relationship, by contrast, is the condition that will prepare us to reflect Christ's character.

behind him, or the one who has failed miserably, falling many times? Who has the greater temptation to rest on his laurels—the one who has them or the one who doesn't? And who has the stronger temptation to go independent, to live life alone apart from God—the one who has power within, the one by divine nature who could be inherently self-sufficient, or the one who was born inherently sinful?

In 1956 my brother came down with the foreign-car disease. He was so enthusiastic that I caught it from him—"great gas mileage, passes anything on the road, rides like a Cadillac," and so on. I bought a Volkswagen, too, and regretted it until I gradually got more of the disease.

Not long after I purchased the Volkswagen with its thirty-six horsepower, I sat at a stoplight about to turn green. Suddenly one of those local smart alecks from the high school pulled up beside me in his hot rod—with four hundred horsepower and four on the floor. Although I had four on the floor, too, I forgot that I had only "four in the furnace." We revved up our engines, the light flashed green, and we headed across the intersection. By the time I got across, he was down at the next stoplight. I've never had the urge to do that since then, because I know I'd lose. When you have the horsepower under the hood, *then* you're tempted to use it.

And what a pitiful comedy it is that we present when, with our little thirty-six horsepower, we continually think we can use it, depend on it, and go about assuming that God will accept the will for the deed because we don't have the time to submit or surrender to Him. No time for communion, no time to allow God to take control of our lives and work in us to will and to do. So we live and operate independently, relying on our thirty-six horse-power, while Jesus, born God, lived His entire life not using any of His personal divine power.

Again, what was the greatest temptation for Jesus? It was not in the realm of doing bad things but in doing whatever He did—miracles, healing, preaching—through His inherent ability. And that's our biggest weakness, too, the one on which we fall, on which we fail all the time.

That's why our personal relationship with God is the beginning, the end, the middle, the sum total—the basis of our Christian life. The individual Christian's devotional life, just as Jesus' was for Him, is the "vital key." It is the method by which we daily submit, surrender, and come under the control of the power of love, letting God will and do within us. According to Ellen G. White, "sanctification means habitual communion with God" (*Review and Herald*, March 15, 1906). Without personal, individual communication with God each day, we cannot get in touch with the love and power He has to offer us.

Jesus had no advantage because of His greater power—because the greater the power, the stronger the temptation. Ellen White comments that "it was a difficult task for the Prince of Life to carry out the plan which he had undertaken for the salvation of man, in clothing his divinity with humanity. He had received honor in the heavenly courts; and was familiar with absolute power. *It was as difficult* for him to keep the level of humanity as it is for men to rise above the low level of their depraved natures, and be partakers of the divine nature" (*Review and Herald*, April 1, 1875, italics supplied). Jesus never had to go through the sinner's struggle whether to *become* a Christian or to continue in sin, but He did have another equally as difficult. Of course, the all-inclusive reason He had no advantage is because the issues are in terms of relationship, not behavior.

Isn't it something that a being who is God acts like man?

And mere mortals try continually to act like God. Christ was familiar with absolute power, and it was at least equally as difficult for Him not to tap it as it is for us to overcome our depraved natures. Can you understand giving up absolute power?

Are there differences in Christ's life? Yes. But did they give Him any advantage over us? No. Then doesn't it follow that Jesus is the greatest possible example of obedience by faith, of surrender and submission, of using the will to come under the control of love?

The remarkable thing about His life was the things He didn't do, but which He had the power to accomplish. "To keep His glory veiled as the child of a fallen race, this was the most severe discipline to which the Prince of life could subject Himself" (SDA Bible Commentary, Vol. 5, p. 1081). "The enticements which Christ resisted were . . . urged upon Him in as much greater degree as His character is superior to ours" (The Desire of Ages, p. 116).

"Christ could have imparted to men knowledge that would have surpassed any previous disclosures and put in the background every other discovery. . . . But He would not spare a moment from teaching the knowledge of the science of salvation. . . . He had come to seek and to save that which was lost, and He would not be turned from His one object. He allowed nothing to divert Him" (Testimonies for the Church, Vol. 8, pp. 309, 310).

"Oh," we say, "Jesus was different. His special role was to seek and to save the lost. That's why He didn't bother with the other sorts of knowledge." But the mission of Jesus is ours too! Maybe I do have the ability to analyze, dissect, theorize, and philosophize, and maybe I feel I've got to demonstrate my mental acumen. But is that necessary? If it is the threat of peer pressure, then doesn't Christ's control free me from that? Do I still have to worry about what others think of my intellect? And wouldn't it be wonderful if in all the departments of our institutions we could have dedicated, godly Christians who would determine, "Whatever my niche, I am going to dedicate myself to one thing—to seek and to save the lost—and I won't allow anything to divert my mind from that."

Whenever Jesus met the temptation to divulge knowledge for knowledge's sake and to dissect and analyze trivia, He never let it turn Him from His one object. "Christ imparted only that knowledge which could be utilized. His instruction of the people was *confined* to the needs of their own condition in practical life. . . . To those who were so eager to pluck from the tree of knowledge, He offered the fruit of the tree of life. They found every avenue closed, except the narrow way that leads to God. Every fountain was sealed, save the fountain of eternal life" (*ibid.*, p. 310, italics supplied).

What would happen in a school in which every faculty member committed himself to that goal? I've seen it happen with some, and I know it's possible—whether it's biology or physics, history or philosophy—to bend all the powers of the mind toward knowing the plan of salvation and of seeing it applied to others around you. I am interested in the age of the earth's matter, but I am much more concerned that when Jesus comes, all of us will leave the matter of the earth behind as we ascend with the saints caught up to meet Jesus. And I don't care as much about the scientific analysis of the ashes of a man burned at the stake as I do about coming forth in the right resurrection.

I have a burden for making Christ first in everything that we do, and I would like to appeal to educators and professional people, parents and children, and yes, even to my fellow preachers—to *all* of you, whatever you do, whoever you are, wherever you may be—to make Christ first in your lives and teaching.

How did Jesus maintain His life of submission to His Father's control? How did He remain in constant dependence upon God? The book *Education*, page 259, tells us that "it was in hours of solitary prayer that Jesus in His earth life received wisdom and power."

"Daily beset by temptation, constantly opposed by the leaders of the people, Christ knew that He must strengthen His humanity by prayer. . . . Thus He showed His disciples where His strength lay" (*Counsels to Parents, Teachers, and Students*, p. 323).

"From hours spent with God He came forth morning by morning, to bring the light of heaven to men" (*Christ's Object Lessons*, p. 139).

All of our theology in salvation by faith boils down again to our devotional time with God, communication day by day. And when we look at Jesus' life, we can see what He went through and what He gave up in order to become our perfect example.

As a child I pulled weeds in the back forty. I don't know why we had to plant that big garden in Modesto, California. At least I should have known better, because I was the one who had to weed it. My preacher father would go out in his evangelistic work somewhere, and he'd send me down to get all those weeds removed before he returned. When I'd go out there under the hot climate of Modesto, with those eternal little gnats buzzing in my ears, the experience would convince me of the truth of Jesus' statement about weeds: "An enemy hath done this" (Matthew 13:28).

But the sting would disappear from my task when my father would come out and pull weeds with me. Since then, I've gotten even with my dad by sending my own kids to weed our garden. But I've seen the light in their eyes and the happiness in their faces when I'd join them. Instead of leaving me to pull weeds in this weed patch of a world, Jesus came on a long trip, not just to die for me, but to show me how to get the weeds out by pulling them *for* me and to keep them from growing through reliance on His divine power.

Chapter 7

How to Handle Temptations

When I have discussed the proper function of the will in living the Christian life, people have often asked me, "Well, I understand that I'm not supposed to fight my own problems—that theoretically if I'm surrendered to Christ, then I can be victorious over sins. But what do I do when I'm hit with a temptation even after I've spent time with God in the morning?" And while some people might think the question confined to teenagers and boys and girls, I have met many kindly white-haired grandmothers and other people who have admitted that it is still a pertinent subject.

What is the proper function of the will in trying to handle sins, problems, temptations? I'd like to remind you, first of all, that if *we* attempt to handle temptations apart from God, we won't succeed. Anyone who struggles to take care of them through his own techniques, methods, and gimmicks will lose the battle. Also, prior to his understanding of the proper use of the will, the amount of willpower that each person happens to have (or that which he lacks) will probably influence his method of handling temptation. You see, the question of how to handle temptations is a composite of all the facets of salvation by faith in Christ alone. It is the personal application of the theory of the proper use of the will in the individual crisis.

101

Now, I don't believe that praying when temptations come will give me victory over them. I've tried it, and it doesn't work. Nor will verses of Scripture or singing hymns. But someone always suggests such methods, and some people try them, only to find that failure and defeat still plague them. They get frustrated and discouraged. Why? They are fighting the battle where it isn't.

As we begin to study this topic, I'd like to remind you that sin is not confined to the area of behavior—doing wrong things. According to Romans 14:23, "whatsoever is not of *faith* is sin." Therefore the greatest single sin (which *causes* others) and the primary issue in temptation is to do anything, right or wrong, *outside of the faith relationship with Christ.* Once we're living apart from Him, from dependency upon Him, then the *sins*—doing wrong things—follow *as a result.* If my problem seems to be with sins, my real difficulty lies back at the fundamental question of whether I am living a life of faith or whether I am relying on my own strength. Scripture gives us some encouragement for real victory, however, for it tells that Jesus understands our problems and struggles.

"Seeing then that we have a great high priest, that is passed into the heavens, Jesus the Son of God, let us hold fast our profession. For we have not an high priest which cannot be touched with the feeling of our infirmities; but was in all points tempted like as we are, yet without sin. Let us therefore come boldly unto the throne of grace, that we may obtain mercy, and find grace to help in time of need" (Hebrews 4:14-16).

The passage declares that we have a great High Priest in heaven—a real live person in human form. What is He doing? He's remembering what it was like to live in our world of sin, and He knows what it means to be "touched with the feeling of our infirmities." When He was here on earth, He was tempted the same way we are today. Now, He didn't have to resist watching the late-late show on television. When the Bible says that He was tempted in "all points," it doesn't mean the little details of temptations that we have today. There's an evolution in terms of sins and temptations and the things that clamor for our attention. And the person who tries to figure out how Jesus could possibly have resisted all the little things that we face today is going too far. I would also like to add that "all points" does not appear in the original Greek. It merely says that Jesus was tempted in "all." But He was tempted to every extent and probably even further than we ever will be.

The clue to understanding the proper use of the will in handling temptations appears in Hebrews 4:16. Before looking further into it, however, let us notice what Jesus had to say about temptation to His disciples in the Garden of Gethsemane just before His arrest and trial. They were getting drowsy, having trouble staying awake. Jesus said to them, "Pray that ye enter not into temptation. . . . Why sleep ye? rise and pray, lest ye enter into temptation" (Luke 22:40-46). Notice the sequence. Pray *now*, before temptation comes *later*.

Matthew describes the same scene with slightly different wording: "Watch and pray, *that* ye enter not into temptation: the spirit indeed is willing, but the flesh is weak" (Matthew 26:41). Some people will conclude, "That's the secret. I'm supposed to watch against temptation, and at the first sign of trouble I'll pray and gain the victory." No, I don't believe that's correct. The sequence is to pray *before* the temptation ever appears.

What was Jesus really saying? "Watch and pray"—*now* —"that ye enter not into temptation"—*later*. We're to come boldly before the throne of grace *now* that we might have help in time of need *then*. I believe that one reason for defeat in our attempts to live the Christian life is that in a crisis we try to draw on reserve power that we don't have. We forget that we don't write a check unless we have money in the bank to cover it. If we do it without adequate funds, it's going to bounce.

The Bible describes the way we should handle temptation. "The Lord knoweth how to deliver the godly out of temptations" (2 Peter 2:9). But you have to be among the godly before He can deliver you. I would like to remind you that it involves more than simply being a member of the church. We should know that much by now. Judas was a member of the church—in fact, church treasurer. Ananias and Sapphira were members. Being godly consists of something more than external morality for a time. It has to include more than paying tithe and being staunch health reformers. Being godly is not possible apart from knowing God and partaking of His godliness day by day.

Would it be safe to say that the Lord can't deliver the ungodly out of temptation? Why can't He? Some people say that God can do *anything*, but I don't believe it. God can't change my life for me unless I respond to Him. He's completely limited when it comes to doing that. Remember, God never forces Himself upon us. We must choose to come under His control of love. And if we do not decide to rely on God, He cannot help us handle temptations. Once we have allowed Him to bring us into the experience of being spiritual rather than just religious, then He can liberate us from temptations. The great God who controls the sun, moon, stars, and all the planets, keeping them from crashing together —the God who can send our world around the sun every year at virtually the exact same time without varying but a fraction of a second, the God who can hang a planet on nothing—that same God can do nothing to change my life unless I let Him.

Often we have gone through the Bible finding promises that we can claim while ignoring the conditions listed there. One such text occurs in 1 Corinthians 10:13: "There hath no temptation taken you but such as is common to man: but God is faithful, who will not suffer you to be tempted above that ye are able; but will with the temptation also make a way to escape, that ye may be able to bear it." Paul here speaks of godly people. (Well, perhaps he was being a little too gracious toward the people in the Corinthian church.) He assumed that his readers knew what it meant to be spiritual, to be godly, to have a faith relationship, even though some of the Corinthians apparently did not. I do not believe that the promise can apply to a person who lives apart from such a relationship. God has to work in dealing with human beings *within the framework of a personal relationship*.

We must always remember two points: (1) The real issue in sin and temptation involves dependence upon ourselves. (2) If I am depending on myself, I'll end up resorting to certain gimmicks and maneuvers to get me out of the crisis of temptation I'm already in, and even then the "victory" is only external. God's plan is for us to resist the primary issue in sin and temptation by fighting the fight of faith—knowing what it means to depend upon God. Then when temptations come, God, instead of me, is able to handle them.

The problem is, however, that the person who is able to handle the temptations outwardly apart from a relationship of dependence only fools himself. But remember, sin and temptation are stronger than any man's willpower, and if I think I have enough backbone to overcome temptations by myself, then I'm deceiving myself. The only thing that I can do is to *appear* victorious on the *outside*. But I've already lost the battle on the inside. True victory is always *from within before the crisis* ever reaches me. It doesn't come at the time of the crisis.

"Well," someone says, "Jesus quoted Scripture, and that's how He triumphed over the devil." No, that's *not* the way He got victory. But He did quote Scripture. It's interesting to read the account of His temptation in the wilderness. "Then was Jesus led up *of the Spirit* into the wilderness to be tempted of the devil" (Matthew 4:1). And that can encourage you when you feel you're on the same track. It also helps to read the words later in the same chapter: "Then the devil leaveth him" (verse 11). And I'm certainly glad for those times of reprieve when the devil leaves me. The trouble is, however, that just about the time I start gloating over that, he's back again. But the devil does have enough sense to know that he can't keep up a constant bombardment. He's going to lose doing that.

So Jesus quoted Scripture, "It is written . . ." We have used the experience to support the idea that we must memorize Scripture to get us out of difficulty. But did Jesus *depend* upon the quoting of Scripture for victory? No!

Have you ever been in a situation where you faced some temptation in which you felt that if you quoted Scripture, it might help—but you didn't because you didn't want help at that point? You know that if you pray, you might receive strength to resist it, so you save your prayer until later when you'll ask for forgiveness. Naturally you're afraid that God might manage to stop you from carrying through with it. I'm speaking from personal experience.

Then there's the kind of temptation in which you don't have any time to pray or quote. Some temptations require careful planning, thought, and premeditation on your part—the long form. But the short form of temptations is quicker. You slap me; I hit you back. No time to quote Bible verses, no time to pray, no time to sing hymns. And if you're ever going to get any help over the short-form temptations, you'll have to have the reserve in the spiritual bank before they ever hit you.

Why did Jesus quote Scripture? Because He had already known its use long before on His knees in secret prayer, and He knew what it was like to have the power of God in His life. The quoting of Scripture came as a spontaneous response to the crisis of the moment. He didn't depend upon mouthing some magical phrases for victory. Rather He relied for victory upon God's indwelling presence, which resulted from the personal, daily relationship with the Father. A person *may* pray when he is tempted, if he is in touch with the Father, and he *may* quote Scripture, and he *may* sing, but that's not what gives him the power to overcome.

True, Jesus told us to watch and pray. But He wasn't talking primarily about watching for temptations on specific things. Rather we need to keep on guard that nothing will separate or keep us from God, from personal dependence, from daily relationship with Him (see *Steps to Christ*, p. 72).

Notice what part we are to do, and what part Christ will do *for us:* "Christ changes the heart. He abides in your heart by faith. You are to maintain this connection with Christ by faith and the continual surrender of your will to Him; and *so long as you do this,* He will work in you to will and to do according to His good pleasure. . . . Then with *Christ working in you,* you will manifest the same spirit and do the same good works—works of righteousness, obedience" (*Steps to Christ*, pp. 62, 63, italics supplied).

If we were to read Hebrews 4:16 the way we've often practiced handling temptations on our own, it would go, "Let us come boldly to the throne of grace *in time of need* that we may obtain mercy." But is that what it really says? No. It reads, "Let us therefore come boldly unto the throne of grace, that we may obtain mercy, *and* find grace to help *in time of need.*"

I have mentioned a bank from which we can draw reserve power. The exceeding riches of God's grace and the grace of our Lord Jesus Christ make any billionaire here on earth look like a pauper. If we know what it means to keep in touch with the Great Banker of heaven, then when the crisis comes, the power will await us. The Spirit of the Lord will lift up a standard against the enemy (Isaiah 59:19).

Someone protests, "Then you're really saying that God can deliver only the godly out of temptation, and so if I fall into temptation, then I'm not godly?" In a sense, yes. You weren't relying on God *at that time*. The Lord knows how to deliver us from temptations *at those times* when we're relying on Him rather than ourselves, even while we're trying to learn what it means to rely on Him or to be "godly" *all* of the time. Just because I fail in a given temptation doesn't mean that I don't still belong to God. What it does indicate, however, is that in some sense, because of my immaturity, I am not resting in His strength then, but upon myself and my own maneuvers to get me out of the crisis. If I'll continue to seek Him, though, regardless of my failures to overcome all temptations, He'll see me through to complete and ultimate triumph.

That's the significance of the verse in 1 John 3:6, which says, "Whosoever abideth in him sinneth not: whosoever sinneth hath not seen him, neither known him." I've heard some say this means we won't sin *habitually*.

What is 1 John 3:6 really talking about? What is the primary issue in sin? It is *not abiding in Him*. Then if I'm abiding in Him, I'm not sinning. Verse 9 of the same chapter states, "Whosoever is born of God doth not commit sin; for his seed remaineth in him: and he cannot sin, because he is born of God." What is the seed? Jesus, the Word of God. If I've been born again, I don't want to live on my own independence. I want to qualify for what it means to abide in Christ, to come under His control of love. That's the basic issue in sin, in any temptation—to do whatever I do apart from dependence on Him.

Remember that God never intended that our sins, our mistakes, or our problems should obsess us. Have you ever tried so hard to go to sleep at night that you have kept yourself awake? It's possible to fight Satan so strongly that you become more like him. God has a better plan. It is for you to look to Him, to know Him in a personal, daily relationship of love and dependence.

"For a long time I tried to gain the victory over sin," W. W. Prescott wrote, "but I failed. I have since learned the reason. Instead of doing the part which God expects me to do, and which I can do [and which He cannot do for me], I was trying to do God's part, which He does not expect me to do, and which I cannot do [and which He has promised to do for me]. Primarily, my part is not to *win* the victory, but to *receive* the victory which has already been won for me by Jesus Christ.

" 'But,' you will ask, 'does not the Bible speak about soldiers, and a warfare, and a fight?' Yes, it certainly does. 'Are we not told that we must strive to enter in?' We surely are. 'Well, what then?' Only this, that we *should be sure for what we are fighting, and for what we are to strive.*

"Christ as a man fought the battle of life, and conquered. As my personal representative He won this victory for me, and so His word to me is 'Be of good cheer; I have overcome the world.' I can therefore say with deep gratitude, 'Thanks be to God, which giveth us the victory through our Lord Jesus Christ.' My difficulty was due to this: that I did not give heed to the fact that victory is a gift, already won, and ready to be bestowed upon all who are willing to receive it. I assumed the responsibility of trying to win what He had already won for me. This led me into failure.

"This victory is inseparable from Christ Himself, and when I learned how to receive Christ as my victory through *union* with Him, I entered upon a new experience. I do not mean to say that I have not had any conflicts, and that I have not made any mistakes. Far from it. But my conflicts have been when influences were brought to bear upon me to induce me to lose my confidence in Christ as my personal Saviour, and to *separate* from Him. My mistakes have been made when I have allowed something to come in between me and Him to prevent me from looking into His blessed face with the look of faith. When I fix my eyes upon the enemy, or upon the difficulties, or upon myself and my past failures, I lose heart, and fail to receive the victory. Therefore, 'Looking Unto Jesus,' is my motto.

"The fight which I am to fight is 'the good fight of faith,' but the weapons of this warfare are not of the flesh. I do not believe in myself, and therefore I have no confidence in my own power to overcome evil. I hear Him saying to me, 'My power is made perfect in weakness,' and so I surrender my whole being to be under His control, allowing Him to work in me 'both to will and to work.' . . . He does not disappoint me. By living His life of victory in me, He gives me the victory" (*Victory in Christ*, Review and Herald Publishing Association, pp. 25-27, italics supplied).

I would like to appeal to the reader to learn what it means to come to God when the pressure isn't on, when the crisis hasn't arisen yet, when the devil isn't facing you with a temptation. That's what Jesus did—He spent those quiet, early hours of the morning with God, seeking strength for the day (*Christ's Object Lessons*, p. 139).

Chapter 8

"One Thing Is Needful"

"Now it came to pass, as they went, that he entered into a certain village: and a certain woman named Martha received him into her house. And she had a sister called Mary, which also sat at Jesus' feet, and heard his word. But Martha was cumbered about much serving, and came to him, and said, Lord, dost thou not care that my sister hath left me to serve alone? bid her therefore that she help me. And Jesus answered and said unto her, Martha, Martha, thou art careful and troubled about many things: but *one thing is needful:* and Mary hath chosen that good part, which shall not be taken away from her" (Luke 10:38-42).

What was the vital thing that Mary had chosen? Do we still need the same thing today? Try to notice a present spiritual application to the Gospel account—something more than a happening of two thousand years ago, something more than the clang of pots and pans in the kitchen. What was the spiritual lesson that Jesus tried to teach to Martha? Mary sat at Jesus' feet. Martha didn't. Mary placed listening to Jesus as her top priority. Mundane cares weighted Martha down.

"Mary was the 'spiritual' type of person," someone comments. "She probably naturally cared more about religion than Martha did." Is that true? I'd like to take you back to the beginning of the story. If we put together all the

111

bits and pieces in the lives of Mary, Martha, Lazarus, and Simon from *The Desire of Ages* and the Gospels as W. A. Fagal did one year at camp meeting, it makes a story that is better than any novel ever written because it contains all the intrigue and drama, and yet it doesn't end in some kind of dead-end street.

The two girls, Mary and Martha, lived with their brother Lazarus in the village of Bethany. Evidently they depended on him to make the living for the family. Their father and mother must have been dead or gone. Both girls were well known, but one—Mary—was more gregarious and probably more stunning than the other. She was outgoing and friendly to everybody. Everybody liked Mary. And whenever they had a church social, potluck, picnic, or even a banquet, they'd always have Mary there.

Now Martha had less of the artistic personality. Mary was probably one of those who needed the sun to come up just right before she could be at her best, but Martha was consistently the same—steady, ongoing, and substantial. Probably she was not as beautiful as Mary, but she was excellent in the kitchen—she loved to spend her time out there concocting new recipes. She probably even taught Mary some of her skills when Mary was around long enough to pick them up. Martha was a good girl, never did anything wrong. Probably her worst sin involved chewing her fingernails when the Mixmaster didn't work. A religious person (as was almost everyone else in Bethany), she'd faithfully attend the services at the synagogue, while Mary would stay home if she didn't feel like going. Martha was religious, but she wasn't spiritual.

A local Pharisee named Simon, one of the church leaders, frequented the synagogue. And here the plot thickens, for Simon got to looking a little too long at Mary at one of the church potlucks, and he decided to get better acquainted with her. He never should have started on his quest, but he stayed with it. Evidently Mary didn't suspect anything at first, for she was friendly to everybody, and everybody loved her. Bit by bit things went on, however, until the day came that Simon, the church leader, led Mary into sin.

Now when a church leader does something like that, the one wronged usually tells the rest of the church that they can just have their religion. And a lot of people have left the church for a lesser cause. In spite of that, Simon evidently had enough psychological pressure or leverage that enabled him to maneuver Mary into keeping quiet about the whole affair. He ended up scot-free, while the experience went deep with Mary, and with her particular background, the guilt was more than she could stand.

One of the devil's traps is to use your guilt as a weapon to make you do worse things. Probably Mary had the philosophy that it must be God's will that she be punished for her sins. And of course, the best way to punish yourself for secret sin is to do it again, for when your guilt increases, you'll feel worse. Believing that God wants you to suffer for your initial sin, you repeat it again and again. It's a convenient form of self-punishment, and it's one that many of us have used. The devil capitalizes on our guilt and our knowledge of the law, and if we let him, he pushes us on down the road into sin until we find we have only one thing left to do—jump off the Golden Gate Bridge—and he's there, goading us on as we leap.

Before long the gossip around town reported that Mary was becoming a "loose" woman. Women would talk about her. "Have you heard about Mary? Watch out for her. Keep your young people away from Mary." Finally things got so bad that Mary decided to leave. She traveled down the mountain to a little village by the name of Magdala, where she later became known as Mary of Magdala.

Probably she tried to find a decent job at first. I can see her going down the streets, checking with the local employment agencies to find work. The laundromat didn't need her, neither did the local drive-in market. The dry-goods stores didn't have any openings. Perhaps she even tried the catering shops, hoping she could use the skills Martha had attempted to teach her, but the caterers didn't need any help either. Mary began to get hungry.

One day the thought came to her, "Well, you know, you're already into it. Might as well stay with it and make easy money. When you've got enough, then you can quit." It wasn't so easy in the long run, however, but she found people willing to pay her price, and she even found a degree of acceptance and friendship. Her life went on for some time until Mary had amassed a great sum of money. But it wasn't safe to keep money around in those days, with no banks to put it in. People usually took their treasure and buried it in their backyards or fields. Mary had neither at her apartment, and she worried about losing her money. When she had been starving, she thought all her problems would end when she just had enough money, but now that she had accumulated some wealth, she found herself fretting continually about losing what she owned. It is the problem of equating *things* and security. No wonder Jesus advises us to seek eternal values.

Then one day Mary saw a camel caravan going through town laden with costly spices and ointment. Why not invest her money in costly ointment? she thought. Perhaps it would be safer to keep that way. So with a great sum of money, she bought one of the most expensive items—an alabaster box of spikenard, which she took back to her apartment and stashed away in her hope chest.

Days went on. She made more money, ate well, and had

"friends" but lacked peace of mind. I have talked with many people who have been trying to live the wild life, only to discover that just as everybody had said, sooner or later things go sour.

Mary was unhappy. Since no one respected her, her self-image could not have been worse. The religious leaders condemned her, and she couldn't escape the feeling of guilt that tortured her and kept her awake at night.

But one day a traveling preacher came through town. Crowds of people went out to hear Him because they'd heard of His mighty miracles. Mary found herself on the edge of the crowd, listening to such words as: "Come unto me, all ye that labour and are heavy laden, and I will give you rest"; "him that cometh to me I will in no wise cast out."

She couldn't believe it, because religious leaders accepted only the good, moral churchgoers, not sinners, prostitutes, and thieves. In fact, she'd heard that the traveling preacher had been having some trouble with the church authorities because He associated with sinners, thieves, tax collectors, and extortioners. But He accepted them as they were. This was almost more than Mary could stand. Hardly able to believe it, she pressed through the crowd after the outdoor service, and right there in the open she poured out her heart to Jesus and told Him of her burden. Remember Jesus' mission—to heal the broken-hearted and to set the captives free? Jesus went to His knees and prayed for her, seeking His Father's presence in her behalf. And Mary was converted on the spot—her load of sin and guilt vanished.

You know, we've often held the idea that conversion is an immediate, complete, absolute, final change of life—that we'll have no more problems from then on. When the problems *do* arise, then we think we haven't really been converted. But remember, conversion is a supernatural work of the Holy Spirit on the human heart, producing *a change of attitude toward God*—instead of being against Him, you're for Him now. Conversion creates in the person *a new capacity* for knowing and loving God. It's the turning-around point, but only the beginning. And we're told we need to be converted every day, not just once and for all. Conversion is also a gift of the Holy Spirit. Nobody can work it up by himself. Many people have failed in trying to know and love God because they lacked the capacity that comes from the initial new-birth experience given by God.

For the first time in her life Mary saw the true character of God—love revealed through Jesus—and she realized she didn't have to punish herself anymore. She no longer had to run away from a God she feared.

I'd like to say that the story ends there and that Mary lived happily ever after. But the truth is that Mary failed, evidently shortly after Jesus left town. Some people would say she backslid, but I'm not sure I can buy that. When you lost your temper after baptism, did you decide you were a backslider? "Oh, well, losing your temper is different!" Is it? Mary slipped. She failed. But for some reason I cannot call her a backslider, because she still had that change of attitude toward God, and her capacity for knowing Him still remained down inside there.

The next time Jesus arrived in town, she poured out her troubles to Him. Again He went to His knees in her behalf, and again cast the devils out of her. Jesus went on His way, but Mary stayed where she was.

When Jesus was not in town, she found it difficult to hold onto the peace she had found from hearing His words and from being with Him. I'd like to say that after Jesus had healed her the second time, she lived happily ever after, but she fell repeatedly. The Bible records at least seven times that Jesus cast the devils out of her. But He *always* accepted her, and His attitude of loving acceptance broke her heart anew. Whenever Jesus came to town, she would go to hear His words, to talk with Him.

Finally one day she learned the secret of salvation by faith. It was the experience that being with Him produced, of sitting at His feet even when He wasn't in town. When Mary learned that, she began to go to her own knees, seeking communion with the Father each day, growing in a relationship with Him. Things began to get better. Why? Because as Jesus comes in, He crowds sin out. No point in trying to stamp it out ourselves. It happens only by Jesus' entering in, for His power then surmounts our weaknesses. That's why Jesus accepts people just as they are. Only *He* can make the changes.

For too long people have told us that we should fight our sins. Remember the principle "By beholding we become changed"? What are we supposed to behold? Our sins? If we gaze at them, we'll become more like them, but if we behold Christ, we'll reflect Him, and sins will finally disappear. Mary learned that rather than dwelling on her sins and failures she should concentrate on God's love.

Things got so much better for Mary, in fact, that she began to get up new hopes about going home. Maybe they would accept her in Bethany now. It would be nice to see Martha and Lazarus again. She packed up her things, including the hope chest with the box of spikenard, and headed back up to the top of the mountain to Bethany.

Her heart beat faster as she caught sight of familiar landmarks. But near the city walls she began to hear a mournful cry, common in those days. Christ's time saw many lepers, and they had to advertise their calamity so they would not endanger others. Whenever someone approached, they'd have to cry, "Unclean! Unclean!" Whether it was a city magistrate or church leader, a pauper or unknown beggar, Jewish society pushed all lepers outside the city walls. It also disfellowshiped them from the church because they considered a leper a victim of the "stroke," the finger of God. And the lepers had to spend the rest of their days sitting by the road in their rags, begging for crumbs until they rotted to death. Mary had heard the sounds before. She shuddered momentarily and continued on her way.

But as she got closer to the gate, she heard a familiar tone or inflection. She looked at the leper and recognized him. It was Simon, the wretched church leader who had led her into sin. Mary pulled her shawl around her and hurried through the streets of Bethany. As she neared her home she tried to regain her composure.

A beautiful reunion took place between Mary and Martha and Lazarus. But the inhabitants of the town were the same kind of people as before she left. Some said, "Good, Mary's back." But more of them warned, "Watch out for Mary. She's a woman of the streets."

"Oh, but she's changed. She says she met Jesus."

"She won't hold out. Watch her."

It was difficult to live down her reputation, but Mary determined to stay, and little by little she began to feel more at home in Bethany.

How did Mary succeed in not letting the gossip get her down? How did she manage to retain her peace of mind? Jesus had taught her the secret—that communication with God each day would bring her power over her problems and worries. How could she communicate with God even when Jesus wasn't in town? Through a meaningful devotional time of Bible study and prayer—talking with God and listening to Him speak to her. She also learned the secret of the Christian witness. When asked about the changes in her life, or whenever she had an opportunity, Mary simply related in her own words the wonderful things Jesus had accomplished for her. And that's what the Christian witness is—sharing with others what Jesus has done for you. And her listeners became interested in meeting Jesus and in getting acquainted with Him too.

One day Jesus and His disciples came on the long trip up from Jericho to Bethany. Martha thought it would be a good idea to invite them over for dinner, because they'd all get a chance to know each other better. And here we began our chapter. When Martha asked Jesus to get Mary to help in the kitchen, Martha worried about making a good impression on Jesus. But Jesus replied, "[Only] one thing is *needful* . . ." It was His statement on the sum and substance, the beginning and the middle and the end—everything concerning the gospel of salvation. Only one thing is necessary in the Christian life, but it's also the one thing that many of us haven't tried yet. That's why the Christian life means so little to many who have tried and failed—they haven't discovered the secret that Mary had learned. What had Mary chosen? It was sitting at Jesus' feet. And whenever Jesus was in Bethany, no one could drag her away from His feet. She sat right there, learning more and more about God, because she knew what she'd been through and how important Jesus was in her life. Sitting at the feet of Jesus is the same thing we need today.

All of the intangible phrases we use in describing the Christian life—coming to Christ, beholding His presence, sitting at Jesus' feet, surrendering to Him, giving Him your heart or your will, inviting Him to take control of your life—we make tangible by three things that we can do. How do we know each other better? By communicating and by doing things together. The same is true in getting to know

God—communication with Him at the beginning of every day through Bible study and prayer. You study about the life of Jesus as given in the Bible, especially in the Gospels, and apply it to your life, your own experiences, your own wants and needs, and then you talk with God about what you've learned. The third method is to share with your friends what you've received from your personal encounter with God, and telling them what Jesus has done for you will make them desire to seek Him for themselves too.

Does it mean that the Christian life requires nothing else except sitting at Jesus' feet? "Won't we do anything else besides reading the Bible and praying?" some might ask. Of course we will. The Christian has plenty of other things to do and uphold: good works, obedience, high standards, doctrines of the church. But all of them will spring spontaneously from the indwelling Lord. Then we'll do more than we ever imagined and will also reach a higher standard than we have ever known or thought possible. All will grow out of one vital thing—sitting at the feet of Jesus. It must be the central focus, the basis and core of everything else, the cause of all Christian experience, the way we respond to God. And many of us don't realize it yet. We don't think the gospel can be that simple. But Mary chose that "good part," as Jesus said, and it wouldn't be taken away from her.

What about Martha? Was it wrong for her to concern herself with the mundane things of life? I'd certainly hate to dine in a home where the hostess didn't have a little of Martha's spirit in her. A wide field exists for Martha-types with their zeal for active work. Martha was good and religious. She even found piety in her busy work, and soon it was easier to involve herself in church activities and projects rather than to take the time to seek God each day. But Jesus showed her that she must *first* sit at His feet, that she also needed to learn the lesson of salvation by faith. Does that mean she no longer had any interest in the kitchen? Remember, control by God never takes away our personality and individuality. But she learned to seek God first, then invite Him into the kitchen with her—and with the pots and pans. As God became paramount in everything she did she began to know Him better too.

And what of Lazarus? *The Desire of Ages*, page 524, tells us that from their first meeting, Lazarus had a strong faith in Christ. He became one of the most steadfast of Christ's disciples. All of them—Mary, Martha, and Lazarus—became close friends of Jesus, and whenever He came to Bethany, He went to see them because He felt at home with them. They were united in a bond of fellowship and love.

"Oh," someone interjects, "I thought Jesus loved everybody. Aren't you saying here that He showed favoritism?" Jesus had favorites and probably still does. I used to think that He cared more for Peter, James, and John than for the others, but let's remember something about Jesus' relationships. He was closer to them by *their own* initiative, not by His. Jesus didn't choose to be partial to them; *they singled Him out*, and there's a big difference.

Let's also notice that Jesus responds to all types of people. He doesn't love just the church leaders and the "good" churchgoers. He loves sinners too. "Whosoever will" may come to Him at any time. Jesus can accept you wherever and whoever you may be, regardless of what you have done or haven't done in the past.

Jesus went on His way. He did a lot of traveling, and He was gone from Judea (where Bethany is) when Lazarus became ill. It looked bad from the start. Lazarus had a high fever—104.5° and it kept going up—105°, 105.5°. He was almost unconscious. Mary and Martha sent messengers to Jesus. "He whom thou lovest is sick." Surely, because Jesus loved them so much, He would come back immediately to heal Lazarus. But Jesus sent back the message, "This sickness is not unto death." They rushed into Lazarus' bedroom.

"Lazarus? Can you hear us?"

"Yes."

"Don't worry, Lazarus. You're not going to die."

"Really?"

"That's right."

"Who says so?"

"Jesus—He just sent word to us—you're not going to die!"

But his temperature kept rising. He was in terrible pain, and just before he slipped into unconsciousness, they said, "It's all right, Lazarus, everything is going to be all right."

"It is?"

"Yes, Jesus says you're not going to die."

"Sure feels like it, though, but I'll trust His word."

And then he died. That must have been hard to take. And the person who doesn't sit at Jesus' feet invariably ends up getting mad at God, accusing Him of allowing all his troubles. But for the one who really knows Jesus, it's different. And despite the shock and grief they must have felt, Mary and Martha did not waver in their faith. They did not blame Jesus for Lazarus' death.

After an unhurried wait of two days, Jesus said to His disciples, "We're going back to Bethany now. Lazarus is asleep."

"Asleep? Well, you don't want to disturb him then. When a man's sick, he needs all the rest he can get. Let's not go back there." The disciples had another reason besides their concern for Lazarus. They'd heard rumors of a plan to kill Jesus, and they were afraid people would be out to get them too.

Jesus replied, "No, I've got to return to Bethany to wake Lazarus out of his sleep."

"Don't wake him up. He needs to sleep."

Finally Jesus said it reluctantly in language they understood, "Lazarus is dead, but I'm going to wake him up."

All of us have suffered from a sense of loss when loved ones die. Many of them have fallen asleep in the past few years, and many more probably will before Jesus comes again. But it's only sleep. And it's not all bad, because of the morning that will come when Jesus returns. It's only a temporary separation, not eternal, and all of us can look forward to a great reunion someday.

Jesus went back to Bethany, and Mary and Martha met Him. Their faith had remained despite their loss. You know the rest of the story. They had the stone rolled away, Jesus awakened Lazarus to life, and the people shouted their plaudits, ready to crown Jesus king. He was the greatest man on earth, and they wanted to worship Him, but not for the right reasons. So Jesus disappeared from the crowd, because that's the way He was.

In the meantime something else happened that I can't explain or understand from a human standpoint. Jesus is a forgiving, loving friend to anyone, even the unlovables. He came up one day to the outside of the walls of Bethany, probably the same route that Mary had taken. And as He neared the gates, He heard the same cry of "Unclean! Unclean!" Because of His great love, He couldn't walk by that kind of people, couldn't ignore them. He walked over to touch the untouchable. The same power that cast the devils out of Mary, that resurrected Lazarus, cleansed the man of leprosy—the wretched Simon.

Feeling that Simon didn't deserve healing, I would have let him rot by the side of the road. Strangely enough Jesus cured his leprosy before Simon had even accepted Him as the Messiah, as his Lord and Saviour, or as anything. I used to think that Jesus would heal only people about ready for translation. But during my years of ministry I've been amazed to discover some people I was sure God would never heal, but He did, while others whom I was sure would be healed, weren't. That's God's decision, and He's wiser than we are. But it seemed incredible to me that the wretched man who had led Mary into sin was now healed even before he had accepted Christ, before he had experienced genuine repentance.

Christ's miracle created a real problem for Simon, because Pharisees *earn* their goodies. They work for their rewards. But Jesus just dropped it in his lap before he even had a chance to merit it. What a blow to his pride! Now he felt under obligation to do a good deed in return, and even to top Jesus', if possible.

I can just picture him after his reinstatement in the town, lying awake at night, wondering what to do. He couldn't stand it, because he was still a Pharisee, still a "works" man. In the middle of the night, perhaps, he came up with a bright idea. "I'll throw a huge banquet in honor of Jesus. He'll be the guest of honor, and that'll be repayment, posthealing." So Simon planned a big feast at his house for Jesus.

Of course whenever a feast took place in Bethany, you had to get one certain person to do the catering—Martha. But when Simon called Martha on the phone, Lazarus answered, and another idea clicked in his mind. If you want to have a worthwhile feast in Bethany, have someone who has been raised from the dead. *That'll* bring the crowds out. It would also ensure fame for Simon, for people would talk for years later about the feast at which both Jesus and Lazarus were guests. So he invited Lazarus, second only to Jesus, as a guest of honor. But guess who he didn't ask.

The night of the feast came. Almost everyone was at Simon's house. But I can see beautiful, gregarious, outgoing, friendly Mary home alone, staring at the wallpaper. She can't stand it. But it's not just the fact that she didn't get an invitation. Her heart breaks more because she's heard Jesus talk about going to Jerusalem where evil men will put Him to death. And she can't stand the thought, for Jesus is her best friend. Not liking the synthetic custom of sending flowers after loved ones have gone, she believes we should give flowers while folks are still here with us. Then she comes up with an idea. She has to see Jesus before He leaves for Jerusalem—one last time before His death. They didn't invite her, but she'll crash the feast. If she sneaks in quietly, no one will ever know.

Rushing into the bedroom, she opens up her hope chest, takes out the alabaster box of spikenard, and hurries down the streets of Bethany toward Simon's house, trying to organize her thoughts into some sort of plan as she runs. When she goes in the back door of Simon's house through the kitchen, where Martha is busy, Martha tries to stop her, but no one can stop Mary. She gets to the doorway of the banquet room, and it's dark inside. Those little olive-oil lamps are burning, and the people all face the center of the room. Now she has her plan worked out—she'll steal softly and low across the floor to the feet of Jesus. Quietly she'll anoint His feet, and no one will ever know. Then she'll slip out back through the kitchen again.

And that's where her plan went wrong. Whenever you open a box of spikenard, it *screams*. Suddenly its scent fills the entire room. All eyes turn to her. She hears the murmurs of the guests as they recognize her, and she gets nervous and begins to tremble. Fumbling with the ointment, she spills it on Jesus' feet and on the floor. That's when she discovers that she'd forgotten something else too—she has no towel or anything else like it with her. Now in those days respectable women wore their hair up. Only a woman of the streets would let her long, flowing hair down, but Mary never gives it a thought. She unpins her hair and wipes up the ointment. Everyone stares and whispers, and down there at the other end of the table, Simon thinks, "If this man Jesus knows what kind of woman she is and yet still allows her to touch Him, He must not be a prophet!" I don't know how anyone with Simon's record could have thought that way, but he did.

At that moment Jesus turned to Simon and commented, "Simon, I have something to say." And Simon got tight stomach muscles and sweaty palms. He'd heard about how the man could read people's thoughts. Simon stiffened, ready to have his mask torn from his face. He expected humiliation at his house, at his feast, in front of everyone. Already he could imagine the gossip that would go around town the next day. As he began to feel the pain and embarrassment, Jesus, in a kind, tender manner, simply told him a story that only Simon could understand. It went through his synthetic exterior and deep into his heart, and for the first time Simon viewed himself as he really was—a rebel, a sinner, a wretch, an unclean man inside and out, a judge of others. And as he saw himself in the presence of Someone who knew what he was really like—but Someone who still loved him, who showed kindness and tenderness in not publicly tearing the mask from his face—his heart broke and he was converted on the spot. He surrendered to Jesus, accepted Him as his Saviour, and acknowledged Him as the Messiah. Jesus got Simon too.

The stories of Mary, Martha, Lazarus, and Simon tell me that God is interested in each one of us, not just the "honest in heart," but the dishonest too. Determined to have everyone, He doesn't give up, doesn't abandon the hopeless. And He loves sinners, cheaters, liars, adulterers, prostitutes, Pharisees, legalists, and nit pickers. Christ loves the good people who never do anything wrong except to stay away from Him, those who rely on their own goodness, those who see no need of Jesus, those who say, "I'm all right, Lord. Thanks for Your concern, but I don't need You. Go out there and help those who really need You." He loves believers who become ill and go to sleep, for He's made provision to wake them up again for eternity. If that's true, and if He loves all of these, then He must love *everybody* today too.

Have you known God's love in your life? God loves you, and He doesn't give up. He's determined to have you, and He's determined to have me. But He never crowds Himself in, never forces His control on us. We have to make the choice to let Him in, but He keeps knocking. If we let Him take over, what happens?

"Nothing is apparently more helpless, yet really more invincible, than the soul that feels its nothingness and relies wholly on the merits of the Saviour. By prayer, by the study of His word, by faith in His abiding presence, the weakest of human beings may live in contact with the living Christ, and He will hold them by a hand that will never let go" (*The Ministry of Healing*, p. 182).

It is my hope at the conclusion of this book that everyone will decide to concentrate on the "one thing" that "is needful." Will you please discover what it means *in experience* to take that thoughtful hour alone with Him at the beginning of every day? And then, keep opening the door and letting Him into your life. Keep sitting at His feet so that He can complete the work that He has started or wants to begin in your life. If you know what it means to sit at His feet, nothing will trouble you. It doesn't mean you won't have problems, but they won't overwhelm you. What others have done to you won't disturb you, and you won't have to lose sleep worrying about the future and the last-day events. Sickness, pain, and heartache won't destroy you, because you'll have a Friend who will walk with you through all your trials.

"If you will seek the Lord and be converted every day; if you will of your own spiritual choice be free and joyous in God; if with gladsome consent of heart to His gracious call you come wearing the yoke of Christ—the yoke of obedience and service—all your murmurings will be stilled, all your difficulties will be removed, all the perplexing problems that now confront you will be solved" (*Thoughts From the Mount of Blessing*, p. 101).